Emotions in Learning

Emotions in Learning

Edited by:
Francisco Pons
Dawson R. Hancock
Louise Lafortune
Pierre-André Doudin

Aalborg Universitetsforlag 2005

Content

List of contributors — 9

INTRODUCTION

Emotions in learning: Understanding and intervention — 11
Francisco Pons, Dawson Hancock, Louise Lafortune,
and Pierre-André Doudin

CHAPTER 1

Helping children to improve their emotion
understanding — 15
Francisco Pons, Pierre-André Doudin, Paul L. Harris,
and Marc de Rosnay

1. Introduction — 15
2. What is the general form of the development
   of emotion comprehension? — 18
3. To what extent are there individual differences in
   the development of emotion comprehension? — 21
4. What are the causes of this development and — 24
   individual differences?
5. What kind of interventions can help children develop
   their comprehension of emotions? — 28
6. Conclusions — 33
   References — 35

CHAPTER 2

How to facilitate the school integration of abused children?   40
Pierre-André Doudin, Francisco Pons, Laurent Pfulg, and Daniel Martin

1. Introduction   40
2. Types of abuse, risk factors and compensation factors   41
3. Choosing an intervention   44
4. An example of intervention   45
5. Results of the intervention   51
6. Conclusions   53
   References   55

CHAPTER 3

Learning to philosophize in preschool: A step toward primary prevention of violence?   58
Marie-France Daniel, Emmanuelle Auriac-Peyronnet, and Michael Schleifer

1. Introduction   58
2. Philosophical material in connection with the body and prevention of violence   59
3. Some pedagogical tips   61
4. Learning to "dialogue" among peers with *The Tales of Audrey-Anne*   65
5. Children's representations of emotions   68
6. Conclusions   70
   References   71
   Appendix   73

CHAPTER 4

Negating emotions is useless, and yet!   75
François Audigier

1. Introduction   75
2. Knowledge at the risk of emotions   76

3. Between reject and recognition, obstacle and support	82
4. Working with and on emotions to acquire knowledge	89
5. Conclusions	95
References	96

CHAPTER 5
Enhancing enjoyment in learning at school 99
Michaela Gläser-Zikuda and Philipp Mayring

1. Introduction	99
2. Emotions	100
3. Emotions, learning and achievement	102
4. Emotions in classroom and instruction	106
5. Conclusions	114
References	115

CHAPTER 6
Opening doors through enhanced decision-making skills: Preparing young adolescents for healthy futures 117
Jeanneine P. Jones and Dawson R. Hancock

1. Introduction	117
2. So who are these kids we teach?	120
3. The backdrop	125
4. Using realistic fiction to enhance social decision making	126
5. Conclusions	134
References	135

CHAPTER 7
The role of anxiety in metacognition in mathematics 137
Louise Lafortune and Francisco Pons

1. Introduction	137
2. Mathematics anxiety: The problem	138
3. Mathematics anxiety: Different emotional reactions	143
4. Metacognition	146

5.	Metacognition and emotional responses	147
6.	Conclusions	151
	References	155

CHAPTER 8

A view on emotions and learning   160
Mogens Jensen

1.	Introduction	160
2.	Emotions in psychology	161
3.	Development of feelings	164
4.	Emotions and feelings resumed	167
5.	Examples	168
6.	Conclusions	175
	References	177

List of contributors

François Audigier
University of Geneva (Switzerland)
Francois.Audigier@pse.unige.ch

Emmanuelle Auriac-Peyronnet
IUFM of Auvergne (France)
emma.auriac@wanadoo.fr

Marie-France Daniel
University of Montréal (Canada)
marie-france.daniel@umontreal.ca

Pierre-André Doudin
University of Lausanne and High School of Pedagogy of Lausanne (Switzerland)
pierre-andre.doudin@edu-vd.ch

Michaela Gläser-Zikuda
University of Ludwigsburg (Germany)
glaeserzikuda@ph-ludwigsburg.de

Dawson R. Hancock
The University of North Carolina at Charlotte (USA)
DHancock@email.uncc.edu

Paul L. Harris
Harvard University (USA)
paul_harris@gse.harvard.edu

Mogens Jensen
University of Aalborg (Denmark)
mogensj@hum.aau.dk

Jeanneine P. Jones
The University of North Carolina at Charlotte (USA)
JPJones@email.uncc.edu

Louise Lafortune
University of Québec at Trois-Rivières (Canada)
louise.lafortune@uqtr.ca

Daniel Martin
High School of Pedagogy of Lausanne (Switzerland)
daniel.martin@edu-vd.ch

Philipp Mayring
University of Klagenfurt (Austria)
philipp.mayring@uni-klu.ac.at

Laurent Pfulg
High School of Beaulieu (Switzerland)
laurent.p@romandie.com

Francisco Pons
University of Aalborg (Denmark)
pons@hum.aau.dk

Marc de Rosnay
University of Cambridge (United Kingdom)
md364@cam.ac.uk

Michael Schleifer
University of Québec at Montréal (Canada)
schleifer.michael@uqam.ca

INTRODUCTION

Emotions in learning: Understanding and intervention

Francisco Pons, Dawson Hancock, Louise Lafortune, and Pierre-André Doudin

This book is the result of the collaboration by scholars in developmental psychology and educational sciences from Europe (Austria, Denmark, France, Germany, Switzerland, and United Kingdom) and North America (Canada and United States). It provides an overview of innovative research on emotions in learning from psychological and pedagogical points of view. Indeed, emotions have recently emerged as one of the main factors of learning. With this book, the reader will achieve not only an understanding of emotions in learning but also propositions for interventions seeking to help children, adolescents (pupils, students), and adults (teachers) to improve their emotional experience and emotion comprehension in the context of learning and teaching. The book is divided into eight chapters. Each chapter is summarized below.

During the past decade, several studies have shown that children's comprehension of emotions is linked with their school integration. This comprehension is a good index for the quality of children's social relationships with peers and adults at school. These studies raise the interesting question of whether it is possible to improve children's emotion comprehension. Although the importance of helping children in this domain has long been emphasized in clinical psychology, there has been little research on this issue in developmental and educational psychology. In the first chapter, Pons, Doudin, Harris, and de Rosnay discuss the possibility of teaching emotion comprehension to typical and non-typical children.

Abuses (physical, psychological, sexual, and neglect) may have a dramatic effect on children's psychological and social development. In addition to social services, school may reduce the negative impact of these abuses. Many studies have shown that good school integration has positive consequences on children's long-term development (e.g., reduction of the risk of delinquency, improvement of professional, and social integration). Therefore, it is important to support the school integration of abused children. In the second chapter, Doudin, Pons, Pfulg, and Martin present and discuss the evaluation of an intervention program seeking to improve the school integration of abused children.

Many authors believe that school may play an important role in the prevention of violence and that interventions must begin as soon as children enter elementary school. In the third chapter, Daniel, Auriac-Peyronnet, and Schleifer suggest that prevention should begin as early as the preschool level. The support they suggest is situated in the perspective of the Philosophy for Children, found in a collection of philosophical stories, The Tales of Audrey-Anne. Its purpose is to stimulate 5-year-old children's thinking and ability to conduct dialogue regarding emotions, body and violence.

School has a strong tendency to encourage the development of rationality and to neglect emotions because they are considered to be suspicious. Emotions carry the risk of unmanageable judgment and make the pupil as an individual who is submitted to his/her passions and therefore incapable of a rational choice. An alternative would admit not to separate emotion and rationality but to recognize the role of emotions in the learning process. In the fourth chapter, Audigier defines different intervention criteria to integrate emotions into this learning process.

In the fifth chapter, Gläser-Zikuda and Mayring report that in the last fifty years, research on learning and teaching has been dominated by cognitive factors. The emotional dimension of learning at school has been widely neglected and mentioned only within theories of motivation. But more recently, a change in learning research has become evident. Psychology of emotion, emotion and learning, and emotional intelligence are becoming important topics in research on learning processes. The ways in which emotions can be influenced during instruction is also becoming an important question for teachers and educators.

The most complex years of one's life are those that surround young adolescence. During these years, young people experience profound physical, intellectual, emotional, moral, and social growth unlike any other years in life. As a result of these changes, many youth experience a significant amount of emotional confusion and discomfort, sometimes resulting in poor decision-making skills and habits. Inappropriate decision-making skills and habits dramatically impact the social and academic paths that young adults travel in later life. In the sixth chapter, Jones and Hancock describe the emotional beliefs and concerns of contemporary thirteen-year-old adolescents. They examine classroom teachers' use of realistic fiction as a curriculum and instructional strategy to guide students in healthy emotional, social and academic directions.

Anxiety can prevent students from exercising all of their capacities and can, in some cases, prevent doing any mathematical reasoning altogether. Anxiety also influences the functioning of metacognition. Certain students feel that when mathematical explanations are given, a veil, even a wall, suddenly appears in front of them, stopping them from reaching the concentration level necessary for understanding what they are being shown. They are thus prevented from evaluating their metacognitive knowledge and from engaging in the metacognitive processes necessary to solve the problems. In the seventh chapter, Lafortune and Pons explain anxiety towards mathematics and its relation with metacognition and present interventions to help students to minimize that negative influence.

In the last chapter, Jensen discusses the relation between emotions, feelings, and learning processes. Emotions and feelings are discussed in relation to evolution, neuropsychology, and theory of attachment. The analysis focuses on the characteristics related to learning found in three empirical cases from literature concerning learning disabilities, teaching of physics, and apprentices in electronics. Points are made concerning co-learning. In addition, Jensen suggests various ways in which students might take responsibility for their own learning processes.

Finally, we would like to thank Nathalie Girardin for her help in the translation into English of chapters 2, 3, 4, and 7.

CHAPTER 1

Helping children to improve their emotion comprehension

Francisco Pons, Pierre-André Doudin, Paul L. Harris, and Marc de Rosnay

1. Introduction

The influence of emotion comprehension on children's well-being (e.g., social and psychological adjustment) and the value of intervention intended to improve children's emotion comprehension have long been acknowledged within the framework of clinical psychology. Nonetheless, those working in educational psychology have only recently become systematically interested in the impact of emotion comprehension on the quality of children's integration at school and in the value of programs intended to develop children's emotion comprehension.

In the same way that children's comprehension of their own and others' intellectual processes has recently emerged as one of the important factors for school success (see works on metacognition, for example, Doudin, Martin & Albanese, 2001), so has children's comprehension of their own and others' emotions (see works on metaemotion, for example, Pons, Doudin, Harris & de Rosnay, 2002). Indeed, children that show deficiencies in their comprehension of emotions are less receptive academically. They can have a negative impact on the atmosphere in the classroom and, in more extreme cases, they cannot be taught. In educational systems that resort to structural differentiation, these "weak" pupils from the viewpoint of emotion comprehension, risk becoming classroom scapegoats and perhaps even being excluded from regular classes (Doudin & Erkohen, 2000; Lafortune & Mongeau, 2002).

Research also indicates a relationship between children's comprehension of emotions and the quality of their pro-social behaviors with classmates and teachers. This relationship has been identified in both pre-school and school aged children; we provide a summary of this literature below. Denham, McKinley, Couchoud, and Holt (1990) showed that young children who better understood the link between emotions and external causes (e.g., feeling happy when receiving a gift or sad when breaking a toy) were also the most popular with their day-care friends. In their study with children aged 3 and 4 years, Hughes, Dunn, and White (1998) discovered that children with more developed emotion comprehension were less likely to have behavioral problems such as antisocial behavior, aggressiveness or limited empathy. Conversely, Dunn, and Cutting (1999) observed that social games involving more co-operation, inter-individual communication, and other positive transactions, were associated with more advanced comprehension of emotions amongst 4-year-olds. In a longitudinal study, Edwards, Manstead, and MacDonald (1984) discovered that 4- and 5-year-old children who were better able to recognize emotions based on simple expressions, were also the most popular with their classmates one or two years later. Similarly, Dunn, and Herrara (1997) were able to link a high capacity for resolving interpersonal conflicts with schoolmates at 6 years of age to superior emotion understanding three years earlier. Furthermore, Cassidy, Parke, Butkovsky, and Braungart (1992) showed that a good level of emotion comprehension in children during their first mandatory school year went hand in hand with popularity amongst classmates. The relationship between emotion understanding and social functioning was also seen in middle childhood: McDowell, O'Neil, and Parke (2000) showed that 9-year-old children (particularly girls) with a good understanding of strategies for controlling negative emotions were considered the most socially competent by their schoolmates and teachers. Finally, Bosacki, and Astington (1999) found a positive link between emotion comprehension in preadolescents aged 11 to 13 years and teacher evaluation of their level of social competence. In sum, the literature documents a robust relationship between children's emotion comprehension and successful social integration. Although the introduction of emotion comprehension in teachers' training and in school programs is still the object of debate (e.g., over instructive and educative school missions), several educational systems have attempted to facilitate the development of such comprehension in pupils over the last few years.

In spite of awareness of the effect of emotion comprehension on children's school integration and the potential value of intervention programs intended at helping children develop their comprehension, there are certain questions that continue to pose difficulties: (a) What is the general form of the development of emotion comprehension? (b) To what extent are there individual differences in this development? (c) What are the causes of this development and these differences? (d) What sort of interventions can help children develop their comprehension of emotions? In this text, we present a review of research from developmental psychology aimed at answering these questions. Better knowledge of development, individual differences, causes, and interventions intended to help children improve their emotion comprehension should contribute to our understanding of the nature and causes of the comprehension deficiencies experienced by some children. Furthermore, this timely survey of the literature should help us develop and evaluate future intervention programs intended to assist children in developing their comprehension of emotions.

This review is divided into four sections. Each section summarizes developmental research that has relevance for educational intervention. Firstly, we propose a three-stage division of the development of children's comprehension of emotions; such developmental description will help teachers conceptualize the capabilities and limitations of children at various ages. Secondly, we examine individual differences in the development of this comprehension. These initial sections enable us to more specifically define the notion of emotion comprehension and outline a norm from which deficiencies in the comprehension of emotions can be identified. Within this framework, interventions aimed at improving emotion comprehension can be more finely tuned: It becomes possible to delimit the intervention's objective with some precision (e.g., does the pupil shows a delay in emotion comprehension and what level of comprehension can the pupil reach?) and to evaluate the effectiveness of the intervention (e.g., did the intervention program help the pupil catch up?). Thirdly, we examine the causes of development, including factors underlying individual differences in emotion comprehension. Finally, we present intervention programs designed to promote children's comprehension of emotions. These last two sections are intended to demonstrate some of the issues concerning the origins of emotion comprehension and associated deficiencies, and to contribute to the development and use of intervention programs within the educational context. Indeed, a better understanding of the causes of slow emotion comprehension development should not only contribute to the construction of intervention tools adapted to these causes but also aid teachers in choosing individually adapted intervention programs. Indeed, teachers are often best placed to select and implement or make referrals for such programs because of their daily contact with pupils and their knowledge of individual sensitivities and circumstances.

2. What is the general form of the development of emotion comprehension?

Over the last 20 years, emotion comprehension in children from 2 to 12 years of age has been the object of a great number of studies that have enabled the identification of nine more or less complex components of this comprehension (Pons, Harris & de Rosnay, 2000; Saarni, Mumme & Campos, 1998 for reviews). Despite this research, a clear conceptualization of the general form of emotion comprehension development from early childhood to preadolescence has been elusive even in the field of developmental psychology. Indeed, most researchers have studied the emergence of only a small number of components, typically just one, in the same children and they have restricted their analysis to either young pre-school children (usually from 2 to 6 years of age) or older school children (usually from 7 to 12 years of age). Within the framework of this chapter, we propose a three-stage division of emotion comprehension development from early childhood to preadolescence. This division is based on a review of literature and recent studies with children aged from 2-3 to 11-12 years of age in which all nine components of emotion comprehension were measured (Pons, Harris & de Rosnay, 2004; Tenenbaum, Visscher, Pons & Harris, 2004).

First stage: The "external" dimension of emotions

During the first stage (approximately 2 to 4 years of age), which is referred to as comprehension of the "external" dimensions of emotions, three relatively simple components of emotion comprehension emerge. At this time, children begin to identify certain apparent emotions and to understand the effect of some external causes and memories of outside events on emotions. From approximately 2 years of age, when language begins to take form, children start to label basic emotions such as happiness, sadness, fear, and anger. In making these identifications, children are not confined to present reality; they can label imaginary emotions and they can talk about emotions that were experienced in the past and may be experienced in the future. Later, the identification of emotion naturally continues to develop; children are able to identify an increasing number of emotions with added subtlety, such as guilt, shame, pride, happiness, disgust, contempt, shyness, and embarrassment. From 3 years of age, children also begin to recognize certain external causes of emotions. For example, they recognize that losing a cherished object can cause sadness and that receiving a gift can cause joy. Children also understand that the external causes of emotion apply in imaginary contexts. For example, they realize that being chased by a monster can cause fear. From around 4 years of age, children also begin to understand the effect of memories on emotions. For example, they realize that the intensity of anger decreases over time, looking at a picture of a lost loved one can cause sadness, or thinking about a positive event in the past can cause joy. For most children, comprehension of first stage components is a necessary condition for the emergence of second stage components.

Second stage: The "mental" dimension of emotions

During the second stage (approximately 5 to 8 years of age) three new components of emotion comprehension emerge that indicate that children have an appreciation of others as intentional agents. This stage can be described as the comprehension of the "mental" dimension of emotions. During this period, children begin to properly understand the role of psychological phenomena such as desire and knowledge on emotions and they start to make a distinction between apparent "external" emotions and experienced "internal" emotions. From 5 years of age, and even between 3 and 4 years of age under certain conditions, children begin to understand the influence of desires on emotions. Whilst children are able to make links between desires and emotions from an earlier age (e.g., they may recognize that someone is happy if they get what they want), they have great difficulty accommodating conflicting desires: It is not until about 5 years of age that they understand that two people in the same situation (e.g., who are both thirsty and find a bottle full of milk) but with different desires (one person likes milk whereas the other hates milk) can experience very different emotions (pleasure and displeasure, respectively). From approximately 6 years of age, children also begin to understand the role of knowledge (beliefs, perceptions, etc.) on emotions. For example, children understand that a person feels sad because he thinks a favorite object has been lost forever when in reality it has just been misplaced. Starting a little later, between 6 and 7 years of age, children also begin to understand the distinction between apparent and real emotions: They realize that it is possible to simulate or hide/dissimulate an emotion. Thus, someone can cry when in reality he isn't sad or smile even if he is unhappy. For most children, comprehension of second stage components is a necessary condition for the emergence of third stage components.

Third stage: The "reflective" dimension of emotions

During the third stage of emotion comprehension development (approximately 9 to 12 years of age), children begin to understand more complex relationships between internal states, states of the world and emotions. This stage can be described as the comprehension of "reflective" dimensions of emotions. Once again, this stage encompasses three new components of emotion comprehension: The nature of mixed emotions; the effect of moral rules on certain emotions; and the possibility of controlling experienced emotions with mental strategies. At about 9 years of age, children begin to understand the effect of moral rules on certain emotions. For example, they realize that a person may feel guilty after doing something morally reprehensible such as stealing a desired object or lying and they also realize that a person may feel proud after doing something morally valued such as resisting temptation or giving something up for another person. Between 9 and 10 years of age, even sooner under some conditions, children also begin to understand the nature of mixed or ambivalent emotions: They understand that a person can simultaneously experience different or even conflicting emotions.

For example, a person can be happy to have found his favorite pet and at the same time sad to find out the pet is hurt. Toward 11 years of age, even sooner under certain conditions, children also begin to understand how to effectively control experienced emotions. For example, they understand that thinking about something pleasant can help a person stop feeling sad, thinking about something sad can help a person stop laughing and speaking about an unpleasant emotion can decrease its intensity.

Emotion comprehension and emotional experience

To conclude, we would like to stress that children's emotion comprehension must not be confused with emotional experience, even if a complex relationship exists between them. Whereas children understand the effects of moral rules on emotion from about 9 years of age, they are capable of experiencing emotions such as pride or guilt before this age (from the first year of life according to some psychoanalyst authors). A further example is that children must reach 6 or 7 years of age before they start to understand the distinction between apparent and real emotions. Nevertheless, from approximately 4 years of age they are able to simulate or hide/dissimulate an emotion, such as smiling when receiving a gift they dislike. To summarize, there is a décalage between children's practical competence and their ability to think about emotions in more abstract or general terms (Meerum Terwogt & Olthof, 1989; Pons & Doudin, 2000; Pons & Harris, 2001 for discussions).

3. To what extent are there individual differences in the development of emotion comprehension?

Most of the work we have reviewed to this point has focused on identifying the average ages at which each component of emotion comprehension emerges. These studies have aimed to capture the universal character of emotion comprehension development rather than recognizing individual differences in this development. Recently, some authors have begun to systematically investigate these differences (Cutting & Dunn, 1999; Harris, 1999, Harris & Pons, 2003; Pons, Lawson, Harris & de Rosnay, 2003 for reviews). One of the basic epistemological postulates of these works is to no longer consider individual differences in emotion comprehension development as measurement errors or random deviations (occurring, for example, because of the concentration, motivation, and fatigue levels of the subject), but rather as the expression of characteristics specific to the child. At least five key findings have emerged from these works.

Early manifestations

Individual differences in emotion comprehension are observable very early in children's development, almost from their very first conversational interactions. For example, the quantity of utterances with emotional content varies enormously in 2-year-old children: Some generate more than 25 emotional reference statements per hour (e.g., 'naughty', 'nice', 'good', 'sad', etc.), whereas others generate none (Dunn, Brown & Beardsall, 1991).

Development

Individual differences in children's emotion comprehension are observable throughout their development, not only in pre-school children (Dunn, Brown, Slomkowski, Tesla & Youngblade, 1991; Hughes & Dunn, 1998; Pons, Harris & de Rosnay, 2004; Youngblade & Dunn, 1995), but also in elementary school children (Pons, Harris & Doudin, 2002; Steele, Steele, Croft & Fonagy, 1999). For example, some children between 4 and 5 years of age have a level of emotion comprehension that is superior to other children aged between 10 and 11 years (Pons, Lawson, Harris & de Rosnay, 2003). Consequently, children's emotion comprehension development is characterized not only by a very important age effect (see previous section), but also by very important individual differences at every age.

Stability

Individual differences in emotion comprehension are stable over time. Longitudinal studies over a one-year (Hughes & Dunn, 1998) and three-year (Brown & Dunn, 1996; Dunn, Brown & Beardsall, 1991) period show great stability in these differences. For example, 2- to 3-year-old children that generate the fewest utterances with emotional content are also those that have the lowest level of emotion comprehension at 6 years of age. Three- to 4-year-old children who most readily communicate spontaneously about emotions are those who show better comprehension of emotions a year later. Finally, the level of emotion comprehension of children at 7, 9, and 11 years of age corresponds to their level of emotion comprehension a year later; there is, of course, a general improvement (Pons & Harris, in press).

Generality

Individual differences in emotion comprehension are not the expression of a specific delay or advantage in the comprehension of emotion (i.e., one or another of the nine components described above). Rather, it appears that children have general delay or advantage across various components of emotion comprehension (Pons, Harris & Doudin, 2002; Pons, Lawson, Harris & de Rosnay, 2003).

Irreversibility versus Intervention

Leaving the family environment to enter pre-school between 3 and 4 years of age or elementary school between 5 and 6 years of age brings on important emotional and cognitive changes, such as meeting new people with whom children will have an opportunity to communicate and participate in new emotional experiences. However, the transition from the family environment to pre-school and later to school does not seem to have a significant impact on the extent of individual differences in emotion comprehension; these transitions neither decrease nor increase such individual differences. For example, young children that have a higher than average comprehension of emotions prior to entering elementary school continue to show a higher comprehension after entering the school system. Continuity of individual differences in emotion understanding as children move through various environments suggests that there may be a sensitive period during which their level of emotion comprehension becomes relatively fixed. Does this mean that at a certain age, around 2 or 3 years of age for example, individual differences in emotion comprehension become irrevocable? In the last section of this chapter about interventions intended at helping children develop their emotion comprehension some elements of response are suggested.

4. What are the causes of this development and individual differences?

What possible explanations are there regarding development and individual differences in emotion comprehension? Today, several explanations are suggested, which may be conceived as being more or less environmental (family characteristics) or individual (children's characteristics) (Harris, 1994, 1999). In this chapter we discuss two of the dominant explanatory models that we identify in the developmental literature: The "affective" and "cognitive" models. While both models recognize the influence of family variables and the particular characteristics of children on emotion comprehension, they nevertheless perceive individual differences in a divergent manner.

The affective model

The affective model places emphasis on children's and caregivers' emotional experience, the basic premise being that emotional experience is one of the necessary conditions, albeit insufficient, for children's emotion comprehension. In early childhood, such a conceptualization of children's emotional development has been dominated by attachment theory because of the importance placed on early attachment experiences for children's emotional regulation. Basic to attachment theory is the assumption that different mother-child pairs come to more or less satisfactory resolutions of emotionally difficult situations (Ainsworth, Blehar, Waters & Wall, 1978). In infancy, these situations usually center on separation issues. Later on, children are thought to rely on "internal working models" of the attachment relationship in order to navigate all manner of emotionally challenging circumstances, especially those involving relational themes (Bretherton & Munholland, 1999; Main, Kaplan & Cassidy, 1985). The child who has a "secure" internal working model carries forward her/his early experiences of sensitive parenting and appropriate responsiveness to her/his emotional needs; effective dyadic emotional regulation in infancy and toddlerhood translates to effective emotional self-regulation in childhood (Sroufe, 1996). Consequently, she/he will be better equipped to encounter and process emotionally challenging circumstances. The child who has an "insecure" internal working model will shun and avoid difficult emotional themes, or become overly "caught-up" in them.

In support of this overall model, children who are rated "secure" on behavioral indices (i.e., the *Strange Situation* (Ainsworth et al., 1978) in infancy or the *Attachment Q-Set* (Waters & Deane, 1985) later on) are better able to take on the emotional themes and describe satisfactory resolutions to emotionally provocative story stems (Bretherton, Ridgeway & Cassidy, 1990; Main et al., 1985). Whilst such stories involve emotional themes, it is unclear to what extent they tap children's understanding of the fundamental nature of emotions as discussed in section 2. Nevertheless, there is some evidence that "secure" responses on such stories are linked with improved emotion understanding on more traditional emotion understanding tasks, such as belief-based emotion (Fonagy, Redfern & Charman, 1997; Meins, Fernyhough, Russel & Clark-Carter, 1998; de Rosnay & Harris, 2002). There is also some limited evidence that "secure" attachment in infancy is linked with children's understanding of mixed emotions at 6 years of age (Steele, Steele, Croft & Fonagy, 1999). Indeed, some researchers have suggested that the attachment relationship and its instantiation in the internal working model, plays a crucial role in children's developing mental state understanding, including their emotion comprehension (Fonagy & Target, 1997).

Reciprocally, other studies indicate a link between the mother-child attachment relationship and the children's emotion comprehension. For example, Steele, Steele, Fonagy, Croft, and Holder (in press) show that there a relationship exists between the type of attachment future parents have with their own parents (measured with the *Adult Attachment Interview*) and, five or six years later, the comprehension their own child has of emotions (comprehension of the role of beliefs on emotions and comprehension of the mixed nature of certain emotions.) The degree of reflection shown by a mother when speaking of her attachment relation with her own mother determines, years later, the level of comprehension her own child has of emotions. These results suggest that the caregiver's emotional coherence and sensitivity fosters a secure attachment relationship with the child; in turn, this relationship fosters the child's emotion comprehension.

In sum, the affective model proposes that the greater the emotional well being of the child and caregiver, the better the child comprehends or will comprehend emotions. In this model, emphasis is placed on children's and caregivers' emotional experience, the basic premise being that these emotional experiences are one of the necessary conditions, albeit insufficient, for children's good comprehension of emotions.

The cognitive model

The cognitive model stresses the importance of children's developing cognitive capacities and didactic social interactions for emotion comprehension. With respect to the latter, several studies show a connection between the manner in which families communicate about emotions and their children's comprehension of emotions. If families, and more specifically primary caregivers, frequently and coherently speak with children about the causes and consequences of epistemic states, including emotions, beliefs, desires, and intentions, a positive effect on children's level of emotion comprehension can be observed. The relationship between family and caregiver discourse variables one the one hand and children's emotion comprehension on the other hand, has been demonstrated concurrently (Garner, Jones, Gaddy & Rennie, 1997; de Rosnay, Pons, Harris & Morrell, 2004), over a period of months (Dunn, Brown, Slomkowski, Tesla & Youngblade, 1991; Ruffman, Slade & Crowe, 2002), and over a period of years (Dunn, Brown & Beardsall, 1991; Brown & Dunn, 1996).

With respect to children's developing cognitive capacities, there is now a large literature showing that children's language skills have an effect on their level of emotion comprehension (Harris, de Rosnay & Pons, 2005). Cutting and Dunn (1999) and Pons, Lawson, Harris, and de Rosnay (2003) demonstrate a clear relationship between language skill and emotion comprehension in children from 3 to 11 years of age; better language skills in various domains (syntax, lexical semantics, and narrative/pragmatic comprehension) correspond with better comprehension of emotions.

In fact, the association between children's language abilities, their conversational environment and their emotion understanding appears to be indicative of a more general relationship between these linguistic variables and children's understanding of mind, which is considered a corollary or even a source of emotion comprehension (Deleau, 1996; Figueras-Costa & Harris, 2001 Peterson & Siegal, 1995). In keeping with this general conclusion, several studies conducted in Australia, the United Kingdom, and France indicate that deaf children show a delay in their ability to differentiate and co-ordinate their states of mind with those of others (i.e., their theory of mind). However, Peterson, and Siegal (1999) underline that deaf children brought-up by parents who are fluent signers do not lag behind in their mental state understanding. In other words, these studies suggest the linguistic influences on children's emotion comprehension are bi-directional: the familial communicative environment impacts on the child's emotion comprehension, but the child also brings her own linguistic competencies to this communicative environment. We can therefore imagine how a positive cycle can become established within the child's social world: children with good language skills have more opportunities to communicate with others more easily and make appealing conversational partners. Thus, they have more opportunity to communicate about their emotions or those of others (Pons, Harris & de Rosnay, in press).

In sum, in the cognitive model, the child's ability to communicate about emotions and the caregiver's remarks on epistemic states are considered more important determinants of children's emotion comprehension than the child's or caregiver's emotional well-being.

Relations between cognitive and affective factors

To conclude this section, we emphasize that it is not easy to clearly differentiate the impact of the factors mentioned in the two models discussed above. Indeed, we can expect the quality of mother-child attachment and the quality of mother-child communication (with emotional content) to influence each other. For example, many studies indicate that mothers who are more coherent when representing their own attachment relationships, presenting a balanced view of their emotional attachments without obvious contradiction, denial or idealization, are more likely to have securely attached infants (van IJzendoorn, 1995). More specifically, Meins, Fernyhough, Fradley, and Tuckey (2001) have shown that mothers who more often make appropriate mental state references to their infants (referring to intentions, desires, emotions, etc.) at 6 months of age are more likely to have securely attached children at 12 months of age. Reciprocally, Main et al. (1985) have shown that attachment is a good longitudinal predictor of the quality of family communication: Securely attached children at 12 months are more likely to engage in fluent, balanced and spontaneous conversation with their parents at 6 years of age.

Finally, the explanatory value of the factors referred to in these two models may not be the same; it may vary according to children's development and also perhaps from one child to another. At certain moments in children's development their emotional experiences and their emotional relations with others may be determinant, whereas at other times in their development it is their caregiver's remarks about emotions or their own capacity to engage in social exchanges that may determine their comprehension of emotions. It is also worth noting that the relative importance of affective and cognitive factors may also vary from child to child and as a function of development.

5. What kind of interventions can help children develop their comprehension of emotions?

There are many studies on the development, individual differences, and causes of children's emotion comprehension. However, research that concerns interventions intended at helping children develop their emotion comprehension, and thus compensate for possible deficiencies in this comprehension, is much rarer (Pons, Harris & Doudin, 2002 for review). To understand how these interventions can be realized, in practical terms, we present three such studies below in a relatively detailed manner.

Interventions with autistic children

Autistic children show a delay in their comprehension of emotions. For example, they find it difficult to recognize emotions such as surprise (Baron-Cohen, Sptiz & Cross, 1993) and to understand the influence of beliefs on emotions (Baron-Cohen, 1991). Hadwin, Baron-Cohen, Howlin, and Hill (1996) have studied the possibility of teaching four components of the first (external) and second (mental) stages of emotion comprehension to autistic children (see section 2 for a description of these stages). The four components of emotion comprehension that were taught within the framework of this intervention were: (a) the recognition of basic emotions (e.g., joy, sadness, anger, and fear); (b) the external causes of emotions (e.g., receiving a gift causes joy); (c) the impact of desires on emotions (e.g., a person will be sad if a wish does not come true); and (d) the effect of beliefs on emotions (e.g., a person will be happy at the thought of receiving a present when in fact he will receive none). Experimental and control groups were compared using a pre-test/intervention/post-test paradigm. During the pre-test phase, children from both groups were evaluated in relation to their comprehension of the four components mentioned above. During the intervention phase, only the experimental group children were taught the components they were unable to understand during the pre-test phase (children from the control group were not taught during this phase). For example, if the child failed in his/her comprehension of the effect of desires on emotions, the experimenter said: "Look, Thomas sees clowns at the circus. He really likes clowns. How does Thomas feel when he sees clowns?" After the child has answered wrongly (because he/she did not understand the impact of desires on emotions) the experimenter added: "Let's see how Thomas feels. Look, Thomas is happy. He is happy because he sees clowns. When you do something you like, then you feel happy!" Finally, the children in both groups were examined once more immediately after the intervention phase and again two months later.

The results of this research revealed a significant and stable development of emotion comprehension between pre-test and post-test phases with autistic children who used the teaching program during the intervention phase. By contrast, there was no noteworthy change in children who did not use the program. Overall, autistic children who used the teaching program immediately mastered an additional component of emotion comprehension and continued to do so two months later. This research illustrates that interventions can help autistic children make up for their deficiencies in emotion comprehension and that the impact of this help is stable over time.

Intervention with young children (4 to 7 years of age)

Peng, Johnson, Pollock, Glasspool, and Harris (1992) studied the possibility of teaching children between 4 and 7 years of age a relatively complex component of emotion comprehension, namely the comprehension of mixed emotions (e.g., understanding that a person can feel happy because he/she found his/her favorite pet, and at the same time, feel sad because the pet is hurt.) Recall from section 2 that it is only around 9 or 10 years of age that children begin to understand the existence of mixed emotions (which may be more or less conflicting) and to correctly understand situations that cause these kinds of emotions. Younger children are either incapable of understanding the fact that experiencing two emotions of different value at the same time is possible or they are unable to imagine a situation that could cause mixed emotions. In order to implement the intervention, an experimental group and a control group were formed and children were tested using a pre-test/intervention/post-test paradigm. During the pre-test and post-test phases, children in both groups were asked: (1) "Do you think you can feel happy and sad at the same time?" (2) "In which circumstances can you feel both happy and sad?" During the intervention phase, only the experimental group children were coached to understand the different situational elements that cause mixed emotions (control group children receive no coaching during this phase). For example, after telling children a story that described how a lost dog found its way home, but was discovered to be hurt, children were asked: (1) "How does the dog's owner feel when his dog comes home?" (2) "How does the dog's owner feel when he realizes his dog is hurt?" and (3) "How does the dog's owner feel overall?" Finally, children in both groups were tested again immediately after the teaching phase.

The results of this research showed significant development in mixed emotion comprehension between pre-test and post-test phases with children who experienced the teaching program during the intervention phase. No significant change was observed in children that did not use the program. During the post-test phase, children that used the program were better at recognizing the existence of mixed emotions. They were also better able to provide examples of situations that cause this type of emotional response than they had been during the pre-test phase. However, this improvement was only observed in older children between 6 and 7 years of age. At 5 years of age the improvement was marginal and it did not exist at 4 years of age. This research demonstrates that speaking about the nature and the causes of mixed emotions can have a positive effect on children's comprehension. Nonetheless, the fact that younger children do not profit from the intervention indicates that teaching comprehension of mixed emotions necessitates some prerequisite abilities.

Teaching children in a school context at 9 years of age

Pons, Harris, and Doudin (2002) examined the possibility of teaching various simple and complex components of emotion comprehension in a school context and the impact of this intervention on individual differences in emotion comprehension. Children tested were 9 years of age on average (5th year of elementary school) and receive regular schooling; none of the children were held back a year or in specialized programs. The children's general level of emotion comprehension was evaluated twice with the *Test of Emotion Comprehension* (TEC[1]) (Pons & Harris, 2000); first during the pre-test phase and second during the post-test phase, three months later. The children were divided into experimental and control groups. During the three-month intervention phase, only children in the experimental group used the *School Matters In Lifeskills Education* (SMILE) (Harrison & Paulin, 2000) teaching program dispensed by their usual teacher on a half-hour a day basis. Control group children did not receive any type of emotion comprehension teaching during this period.

The TEC provides a general measure of emotion comprehension in children from 2-3 years of age to adolescence. It measures nine components of emotion comprehension: (1) categorization of basic emotions (joy, sadness, anger, etc.), (2) the influence of external causes on emotions, (3) the effect of memory on emotions, (4) the role of desires on emotions, (5) the effect of knowledge (belief, ignorance) on emotions, (6) the distinction between an apparent emotion and an experienced emotion, (7) the possibility of controlling an experienced emotion, (8) mixed emotions, and (9) the role of morals on emotions. The more components the child masters, the higher is the child's general level of emotion comprehension.

The objective of the SMILE intervention program is to help children develop their comprehension of the nature, causes, and consequences of emotions. It can be used with children from 4 to 12 years of age and is divided in four parts: (1) Self, (2) Family, (3) Friends, and (4) Others. In each part, several themes are addressed including emotion comprehension. SMILE suggests a certain number of activities to help children develop their comprehension of emotions: (1) relate past and present emotions, and attempt to understand their source; (2) identify people that are liked and disliked; (3) understand the nature of a real or an imaginary friend; (4) recognize and express positive and negative emotions and understand their source; (5) understand the distinction between apparent and experienced emotion and the social usefulness of pretending; (6) identify sources of sadness, anger, and fear and learn to manage them; (7) identify emotions in situations of loss, separation, abandonment, exclusion, and harassment, and learn to manage them; (8) identify and understand sources of pride and guilt; (9) identify what we like and dislike in ourselves and in others; (10) identify similarities and differences in emotions experienced by various people and understand the source of these differences; (11) place themselves in a mistreated person's place and identify what this person experiences; (12) identify the influences and consequences of drugs on emotions; (13) understand how adolescence can influence emotions (e.g., the experience of desires, depression, rage, omnipotence, etc.) and how to manage this change. These activities can be carried out either on an individual or group basis. They can consist of readings and discussions or role-play. SMILE is a mixed teaching program; it attempts to provoke emotions in children, in the here and now, and to remind them of past emotions. It also encourages children to speak and think about their own emotions or those of others, whether they are real or imaginary, past, present or future.

Two results emerged from this research. Firstly, there was a significant development of the general level of emotion comprehension in children that use the SMILE program and no significant development in children that do not use this program. Most of the children that used the SMILE program (83 %) improved their overall emotion comprehension, whereas relatively few children who did not use the SMILE program improved (22 %). Among the children that used the SMILE program and showed progress, 60 % mastered at least one more component of emotion comprehension, whereas 40 % mastered two more. This progress is not trivial. In pre-test, the general level of emotion comprehension in both groups of children was similar to that observed in previous research with children between 8 and 9 years of age (level 7 on average). In post-test, the general level of emotion comprehension in children that used the SMILE program was similar to that observed in previous studies with children between 10 and 11 years of age (level 8 on average). Secondly, individual differences in emotion comprehension were profound in both groups during pre-test; there was a dispersion of answers between 5 levels. During post-test, the spectrum of individual differences remained the same in children that did not use the SMILE program but decreased, although not significantly, in children that used the SMILE program (from 5 to 3 levels of dispersion). However, during post-test, weaker children who used the SMILE program showed a general level of emotion comprehension (level 7) that was equivalent to the majority of typically developing 9-year-olds; they no longer lagged behind their age group. This was not the case for weaker children who did not use the SMILE program; during the post-test phase they maintained a general level of emotion comprehension (level 5) that was below the majority of typically developing 9-year-olds (level 6 on average).

This research demonstrates that in a regular schooling context, a teacher can help children develop their general level of emotion comprehension. This research also shows that an intervention program such as SMILE only has a relative impact on the spectrum of individual differences in emotion comprehension: Children that showed a deficit in their general level of emotion comprehension maintain a level that is inferior to their classmates' average after the intervention. After the intervention, however, these children show a general level of emotion comprehension that is equivalent to the average in their age group; they no longer show a delay or a deficiency.

6. Conclusion

Through adequate intervention, it is possible to help children develop their comprehension of emotions. Furthermore, individual differences in this comprehension are not irrevocable in spite of the facts that they (i) appear fairly early in children's development, (ii) are present all along their development, (iii) are stable over time, and (iv) are general rather than particular to a delay (or progress) in comprehension of some specific aspects of emotions. Schools can play a significant role in the development of children's emotion comprehension, in spite of the fact that this comprehension is determined in part by certain characteristics of children (e.g., linguistic skills, theory of mind ability, attachment relationship to the mother, etc.) and by their family environment (e.g., discourse about emotions, history of emotional attachments, etc.).

We conclude, however, with two important reservations. Firstly, it is not possible to say which aspect of the SMILE intervention program has an effect on children emotion comprehension. Indeed, because of its structure, SMILE is a mixed intervention program in which children both experience emotions and are made to reflect on these emotions. Therefore, it is difficult to say whether emotion comprehension develops because of the experience of emotions, in line with the affective model, or because of the reflection on emotions, in line with the cognitive model. Secondly, it is one thing to show that helping children develop their comprehension of emotions is possible, but it is another to show the effect of this help on pro-social behaviors (e.g., popularity with peers, ability to manage emotions that are too intense or negative, or conflict management), these behaviors being of primary importance for school integration (see the introduction for a discussion). To our knowledge, no empirical answer has yet been given to this problem. There are many studies that indicate a relationship between children's emotion comprehension and their pro-social behaviors, but the direction of this relationship has remained elusive. Do pro-social behaviors determine emotion comprehension or is the reverse true? Is the direction of this relation the same according to each child's level of development or does it vary from one child to another (Meerum Terwogt & Olthof, 1989; Pons & Doudin, 2000; Pons & Harris, 2001)? Here again, we encounter opposition between those who support cognitive versus affective models of individual differences in emotion comprehension development.

Throughout this chapter, we focused on (i) children's emotion comprehension, (ii) the effect of this comprehension on pro-social behaviors and school integration, (iii) the development of this comprehension, (iv) individual differences in development, (v) causes of development and individual differences, and (vi) interventions intended at helping children to develop emotion comprehension. We know that the didactic pupil-teacher link has an important emotional dimension. Consequently, we would underline the importance of focusing in the future on teacher emotion comprehension in professional circumstances and on the possible influence of this comprehension on the development of emotion comprehension in their pupils.

References

Ainsworth, M. D. S., Blehar, M. C., Waters, E., & Wall, S. (1978). *Patterns of attachment: A psychological study of the Strange Situation.* Hillsdale: Lawrence Erlbaum Associates.

Baron-Cohen, S. (1991). Do people with autism understand what causes emotion? *Child Development, 62,* 385-395.

Baron-Cohen, S., Sptiz, A., & Cross, P. (1993). Do children with autism recognize surprise? *Cognition and Emotion, 7,* 507-516.

Bosacki, S., & Astington, J. (1999). Theory of mind in preadolescence: Relations between social understanding and social competence. *Social Development, 8,* 237-255.

Bretherton, I., & Munholland, K. A. (1999). Internal working models in attachment relationships: A construct revisited. In J. Cassidy & P. R. Shaver (Eds.), *Handbook of attachment: Theory, research and clinical applications* (pp. 89-111). London: The Guilford Press.

Bretherton, I., Ridgeway, D., & Cassidy, J. (1990). Assessing internal working models of attachment relationship. In T. Greenberg, D. Ciccehetti & E. Cummings (Eds.), *Attachment in the preschool years* (pp. 273-308). Chicago: University of Chicago Press.

Brown, J.R., & Dunn, J. (1996). Continuities in emotion understanding from three to six years. *Child Development, 67,* 789-802.

Cassidy, J., Parke, R., Butkovsky L., & Braungart, J. (1992). Family-peer connections: The roles of emotional expressiveness within family and children's understanding of emotions. *Child Development, 63,* 603-618.

Cutting, A., & Dunn, J. (1999). Theory of mind, emotion understanding, language, and family background: Individual differences and interrelations. *Child Development, 70,* 853-865.

Deleau, M. (1996). L'attribution d'états mentaux chez des enfants sourds and entendants: une approche du rôle de l'expérience langagière sur une théorie de l'esprit. *Bulletin de Psychologie, 427,* 48-56.

Denham, S., McKinley, M., Couchoud, E., & Holt, R. (1990). Emotional and behavioral predictors of preschool peer ratings. *Child Development, 61,* 1145-1152.

Doudin, P.-A., & Erkohen, M. (Eds.) (2000). *Violence à l'école: fatalité ou défi?* Brussels: De Boeck.

Doudin, P.-A., Martin D., & Albanese, O. (Eds.) (2001). *Métacognition et éducation* : théorie et pratique. Bern: Peter Lang.

Dunn, J., Brown, J., & Beardsall, L. (1991). Family talk about feeling states and children's later understanding of other's emotions. *Developmental Psychology, 27,* 448-455.

Dunn, J., Brown, J., Slomkowski, C., Tesla, C., & Youngblade, L. (1991). Young children's understanding of other people's feelings and beliefs: Individual differences and their antecedents. *Child Development, 62,* 1352-1366.

Dunn, J., & Cutting, A. (1999). Understanding others, and individual differences in friendship interactions in young children. *Social Development, 8,* 201-219.

Dunn, J., & Herrera, C. (1997). Conflict resolution with friends, siblings and mothers: A developmental perspective. *Aggressive Behavior, 23,* 343-357.

Edwards, R., Manstead, A., & MacDonald, C. (1984). The relationship between children's sociometric status and their ability to recognize facial expressions of emotions. *European Journal of Social Psychology, 14,* 235-238.

Figueras-Costa, B., & Harris, P. L. (2001). Theory of mind development in deaf children: A non-verbal test of false-belief understanding. *Journal of Deaf Studies and Deaf Education, 6,* 92-102.

Fonagy, P., Redfern, S., & Charman, T. (1997). The relationship between belief-desire reasoning and a projective measure of attachment security (SAT). *British Journal of Developmental Psychology, 15,* 51-61.

Fonagy, P., & Target, M. (1997). Attachment and the relfective function: Their role in self-organisation. *Development and Psychopathology, 9,* 679-700.

Garner, P., Jones, D., Gaddy, G., & Rennie, K. (1997). Low-income mothers' conversations about emotions and their children's emotional competence. *Social Development, 6,* 37-52.

Hadwin, J., Baron-Cohen, S., Howlin, P., & Hill, K. (1996). Can we teach children with autism to understand emotions, beliefs, or pretence? *Development and Psychopathology, 8,* 345-365.

Harris, P. L. (1994). The child's understanding of emotion: Developmental changes and the family environment. *Journal of Child Psychology and Psychiatry, 35,* 3-28.

Harris, P. L. (1999). Individual differences in understanding emotion: The role of attachment status and psychological discourse. *Attachment and Human Development, 1,* 307-324.

Harris, P. L., & Pons, F. (2003). Perspectives actuelles sur le développement de la compréhension des émotions chez l'enfant. In J.-M. Colletta & A.

Tcherkassof (Eds.), Les émotions. *Cognition, langage et développement* (pp. 209-228). Sprimont: Mardaga.

Harris, P.L., de Rosnay, M., & Pons, F. (2005). Language and children's understanding of mental states. *Current Directions in Psychological Sciences, 14*(2), 69-73.

Harrison, P., & Paulin, G. (2000). *School Matters in Lifeskills Education. a Framework for PSHE and Citizenship in Primary Schools.* Oxford: Oxford County Council.

Hughes, C., & Dunn, J. (1998). Understanding mind and emotion: Longitudinal associations with mental-state talk between young friends. *Developmental Psychology, 34*, 1026-1037.

Hughes, C., Dunn, J., & White, A. (1998). Trick or treat? Uneven understanding of mind and emotion and executive dysfunction in "hard-to-manage" preschoolers. *Journal of Child Psychology and Psychiatry, 39*, 981-994.

van IJzendoorn, M.H. (1995). Adult attachment representations, parental responsiveness, and infant attachment: A meta-analysis on the predictive validity of the adult attachment interview. *Psychological Bulletin, 117*, 387-403.

Lafortune, L., & Mongeau, P. (Eds.) (2002). *L'affectivité dans l'apprentissage.* Sainte-Foy: Presses de l'Université du Québec.

McDowell, D., O'Neil, R., & Parke, R. (2000). Display rule application in a disappointing situation and children's emotional reactivity: Relations with social competences. *Merril Palmer Quarterly, 46*, 306-324.

Main, M., Kaplan, N., & Cassidy, J. (1985). Security in infancy, childhood and adulthood: a move to the level of representation. In I. Bretherton & E. Waters (Eds.), Growing points of attachment theory and research (pp. 66-104). *Monographs of the Society for Research in Child Development, 50*, (1-2, Serial No. 209).

Meerum Terwogt, M., & Olthof, T. (1989). Awareness and self-regulation of emotion in young children. In C. Saarni & P. Harris (Eds.), *Children's understanding of emotion* (pp. 209-234). Cambridge: Cambridge University Press.

Meins, E., Fernyhough, C., Fradley, E., & Tuckey, M. (2001). Rethinking maternal sensitivity: Mothers' comments on infants' mental processes predict security of attachment at 12 months. *Journal of Child Psychology and Psychiatry, 42*(5), 637-648.

Meins, E., Fernyhough, C., Russell, J., & Clark-Carter, D. (1998). Security of attachment as a predictor of symbolic and mentalising abilities: A longitudinal study. *Social Development, 7*, 1-24.

Peng, M., Johnson, C., Pollock, J., Glasspool, R., & Harris, P.L. (1992). Training young children to acknowledge mixed emotions. *Cognition and Emotion, 6*, 387-401.

Peterson, C., & Siegal, M. (1995). Deafness, conversation and theory of mind. *Journal of Child Psychology and Psychiatry, 36*, 459-474.

Peterson, C., & Siegal, M. (1999). Representing inner worlds: Theory of mind in autistic, deaf and normal hearing children. *Psychological Science, 10,* 126-129.

Pons, F., & Doudin, P.-A. (2000). Niveaux de conscience et développement: entre métacognition et méta émotion. In C. Vogel & E. Thommen (Eds.), *Lire les passions* (pp. 111-132). Bern: Peter Lang.

Pons, F., Doudin, P.-A., Harris, P. L., & de Rosnay, M. (2002). Métaémotion et intégration scolaire. In L. Lafortune & P. Mongeau (Eds.), *L'affectivité dans l'apprentissage (7-28)*. Sainte-Foy: Presses de l'Université du Québec.

Pons, F., & Harris, P. L. (2000). *Test of Emotion Comprehension – TEC.* Oxford: University of Oxford.

Pons, F., & Harris, P. L. (2001). Piaget's conception of the development of consciousness: An examination of two hypotheses. *Human Development, 44,* 220-227.

Pons, F., & Harris, P. L. (in press). Longitudinal change and longitudinal stability of individual differences in children's emotion understanding. *Cognition and Emotion.*

Pons, F., Harris, P. L., & Doudin, P.-A. (2002). Teaching emotion understanding. *European Journal of Psychology of Education, 17*(3), 293-304.

Pons, F., Harris, P. L., & de Rosnay, M. (2000). La compréhension des émotions chez l'enfant. *Psychoscope, 21,* 29-32.

Pons, F., Harris, P. L., & de Rosnay, M. (2004). Emotion comprehension between 3 and 11 years: Developmental periods and hierarchical organizations. *European Journal of Developmental Psychology, 1*(2), 127-152.

Pons, F., Harris, P., & de Rosnay, M. (in press). Theory of mind in children: Impact of children's language and families' conversation. In C. Jantzen & T. Thellesen (Eds.), *Videnskabelig begrebsdannelse.* Aalborg: Aalborg Universitrtsforlag.

Pons, F., Lawson, J., Harris, P. L., & de Rosnay, M. (2003). Individual differences in children's emotion understanding: Effects of age and language. *Scandinavian Journal of Psychology, 44*(4), 345-351.

de Rosnay, M., & Harris, P. L. (2002). Individual differences in children's understanding of emotion: The roles of attachment and language. *Attachment and Human Development, 4*(1), 39-54.

de Rosnay, M., Pons, F., Harris, P. L., & Morrell, J. M. B. (2004). A lag between understanding false belief and emotion attribution in young children: Relationships with linguistic ability and mothers' mental-state language. *British Journal of Developmental Psychology, 22,* 197-218.

Ruffman, T., Slade, L., & Crowe, E. (2002). The relation between children's and mother's mental state language and theory-of-mind understanding. *Child Development, 73*(3), 734-751.

Saarni, C., Mumme, D., & Campos, J. (1998). Emotional development: Action, communication, and understanding. In W. Damon and N. Eisenberg (Eds.), *Handbook of Child Psychology, Vol. 3. Social, Emotional and Personality Development* (pp. 237-309). New York: John Wiley.

Sroufe, L. A. (1996). *Emotional development*. Cambridge: Cambridge University Press.

Steele, H., Steele, M., Croft, C., & Fonagy, P. (1999). Infant-mother attachment at one year predicts children's understanding of mixed emotions at six years. *Social Development, 8*, 161-178.

Steele, H., Steele, M., Fonagy, P., Croft, C., & Holder, J. (in press). *Attachment predictors of children's understanding of emotion and mind in the sixth year.*

Tenenbaum, H., Visscher, P., Pons, F., & Harris, P. (2004). Emotion understanding in Quechua children from an agro-pastoralist village. *International Journal of Behavioral Development, 28*(5), 471-478.

Waters, E., & Deane, D. (1985). Defining and assessing individual differences in attachment relationships: Q-methodology and the organization of behavior in infancy and early childhood. In I. Bretherton & E. Waters (Eds.), Growing points of attachment theory and research. *Monographs of the Society for Research in Child Development, 50* (1-2, Serial No. 209).

Youngblade, L., & Dunn, J. (1995). Individual differences in young children's pretend play with mother and sibling: Links to relationships and understanding of other people's beliefs and feelings. *Child Development, 66*, 1472-1492.

---

[1] TEC has been translated into English, French, Spanish, Italian, Dutch, Quichua, Danish, Arabic, German and Greek.

CHAPTER 2

How to facilitate the school integration of abused children?

Pierre-André Doudin, Francisco Pons, Laurent Pfulg, and Daniel Martin

1. Introduction

Different types of abuse can profoundly affect children's intellectual, emotional, social, and even physical development. Measures of help and protection, set up by specialized services to stop causes of abuse, and schools, in collaboration with specialists that work in the school system, are among the bodies that can contribute to reducing problems induced by abuse (Doudin & Erkohen-Marküs, 2000). As shown by Cicchetti, Toth, and Hennessy (1993) in their study on abused children, successful school integration represents an important organizing factor of development, with long-term positive effects such as a decrease in delinquency risks and an increase in the chances of professional and social integration. Thus, all possible steps should be taken to favor school integration of abused children.

The objective of this chapter is to present and evaluate an intervention plan intended to reinforce the quality of school integration for children placed in a specialized institution (boarding school) as a result of severe abuse in their family environment. Rather than resorting to specialized teaching within the institution, and at the risk of reinforcing a feeling of exclusion or marginalization (Doudin, 1996), the institution opted for the children to be integrated in a regular school. However, with respect to the school structure, although this establishment was essentially comprised of regular classes, it also had a few classes for pupils with academic difficulties.

2. Types of abuse, risk factors, and compensation factors

Specialized literature (e.g., Christoffel, et al., 1992) generally defines four categories of abuse: (1) Physical abuse: such as hitting a person; (2) Sexual abuse: such as incest, rape or attempted rape, fondling, exposure to indecent acts or pornography; (3) Psychological abuse: such as verbal discredit or any form of depreciation, and (4) Neglect: lack of care that causes damage to children's psychological or physical health.

These different types of abuse can have serious consequences on children's development and school integration (Erkohen-Marküs & Doudin, 2000, 2001a, for details). Studies on the effects of *physical abuse* underline the difficulties that children may experience managing their aggressiveness (e.g., uncontrolled outbursts of anger) which, in turn, influence quality of relations with peers and teachers. Children victims of physical abuse often manage to associate their successes to their own behavior; however, they generally impute their failures to external and uncontrollable causes, in other words causes that they themselves cannot influence. This type of attribution may then negatively affect their intellectual development and school integration. They also present an absence of normal intellectual curiosity which can be related to lack of stimulation in their family environment (scarcity of interactions). This leads to delays in basic learning (e.g., mathematics and reading). Poor results in school will, in turn, exert a negative influence on self-esteem. A feeling of uneasiness takes root within the school context: the child having become "un-teachable" and the teacher having become frustrated.

In cases of *sexual abuse*, children live a strange situation. They cannot compare their actual experience to that of peers and, socially, they feel atypical. These children are noticeable by their excessive interest in sexuality (sexualized games, seduction, sexually aggressive behavior, and inappropriate sexual knowledge for their age). Such behavior may occasion punishments from teachers and even cause children to suffer rejection from their classmates and teacher. These children often manifest pronounced dependence towards their teacher, constantly searching for their help and their physical proximity, when, in general, the teacher's role is to work on different ways to guide children towards autonomy. This may result in awkward pupil-teacher communication.

Psychological abuse represents the most pernicious and destructive form of violence. Children manifest violent and anti-social behavior, withdrawal into the self, develop poor self-esteem, and run a high risk of developing depression. They demonstrate more attachment which can be a sign of great insecurity and present important academic difficulties, lack of creativity, discipline problems in class, and hostile and angry behavior. Their cognitive development appears to be particularly problematic (e.g., attention and memorization difficulties). Children exposed to family violence manifest more behavior problems in class and higher school absenteeism which makes the teacher's task difficult, even impossible in the case of absenteeism.

Neglect is some children's daily lot. Life with adults that are uninterested in them, that are not preoccupied by their security and that oftentimes reject them leaves little room for intellectual learning. Furthermore, these children primarily search for security, particularly in withdrawal and isolation. This general tendency to withdraw leads to a decrease in learning and socialization opportunities which disrupts their intellectual and socio-affective development. Moreover, negligent parents voice more negative comments about children's behavior. This reveals the quality of interactions which such parents establish with their children – not taking into consideration their development stage, potentials, needs, and specific desires. Children are faced with adults that are inconstant in their moods, uneven in their interaction style and contradictory in the messages they express.

Whatever the type of abuse children are subjected to, their family environment is generally chaotic: divorce, relocation, remarriage, unemployment, and mental illness in parents are often found in abusive families. Children then have trouble finding reference points or the support necessary to construct their personality. They are vulnerable and fragile; their self-esteem is low; they find it difficult to face unexpected events and, because they are accustomed to little predictability in their environment, they spend much energy attempting to anticipate what will happen to them. Parents of abused children were often abused when they were children. Abused children risk integrating a violent model of interaction; they may then also become abusive children and, later, abusive parents. This is the vicious circle of intergenerational transmission of violence (Egeland & Susman-Stillman, 1996).

To apprehend the full complexity of a given situation, one must not only take into account risk factors of abuse on children's development, but also compensation factors (Belsky, 1980; Cicchetti & Rizley, 1981; Kaufman & Zigler, 1989). Thus, even if children have been abused, they can develop their social and intellectual abilities and their critical thinking; they can become confident and competent adults and break the vicious circle of violence and intergenerational transmission. Werner and Smith (1992) note three compensation factors concerning the quality of social support provided to such children. These compensation factors can be adopted, in particular, within the school context: (1) Warm support relationships; (2) Positive expectations on the part of adults, and (3) Sense of belonging to a community.

Adults that were abused as children often report a teacher as having played a positive support role. Teachers not only play a role as knowledge transmitters but also as positive identification models. For Lynch and Cicchetti (1992), a positive and reassuring relationship with a teacher can compensate, at least in part, for a negative parent-child relationship and improve the representation children have of others and of themselves. Children can generalize this new relational approach by applying it to other contexts outside the classroom. The interest shown by schools and teachers to children who feel disinvested is therefore essential. By actualizing essential needs, such as respect, support and solidarity, and by cultivating a sense of belonging rather than exclusion from the school community, schools, and specialized institutions responsible for at-risk children can also compensate for certain deficiencies in children that have experienced an abusive environment (Erkohen-Marküs et Doudin, 2001b). However, and as observed by Lynch and Cicchetti (1992), teachers and headmasters are not always aware of the important role they can play or of their ability to improve a given situation (see also, Pons, Doudin, Harris & de Rosnay, 2002; Pons, Harris & Doudin, 2002).

Nevertheless, not everything depends upon schools' and specialized institutions' ability to assume these compensation factors. On the one hand, families of origin, although they face great difficulties, have abilities and resources which ought to be mobilized rather than denied at the risk of aggravating their troubles. On the other hand, children are "resilient", in other words they have the ability to face stress and adversity and to take advantage of positive elements in their environment (Rutter, 1989; Cyrulnik, 1999).

3. Choosing an intervention

To help abused children with academic difficulties, to enable them to make up for deficiencies and to improve their self-image, teachers must resort to usual school resources, such as academic support, holding pupils back a year or placing them in parallel classes for pupils with difficulties. However, these types of help seem to generate similar negative effects for the majority of pupils (Doudin, 1996, for details): (1) A labeling effect: children are marked by the institution, they become a "case" and, perhaps unconsciously, adults and children themselves will see to it that reality is true to the label ("Pygmalion" effect: see Mingat, 1991); (2) Undermining socio-affective development: these types of help stigmatize children and cause a decrease in self-esteem and in the motivation to learn which in turn can lead to a "learned feeling of powerlessness." In other words, after repetitive academic failures, pupils believe that no matter what they do, it cannot amount to anything (Seligman, 1991); these first two points can lead to: (3) A drop in academic results (Friend, 1988; Will, 1986; Mingat, 1991).

It is not surprising that all of these different aid measures generate the same harmful effects. Indeed, they rest upon the paradox that consists of wanting to integrate pupils academically while cutting them off from their age group (holding them back a year), or removing them from regular class (momentarily for a remedial class, on a long-term basis, or even definitely to place them in a class for pupils with difficulties) (Doudin, 1996.) These measures of exclusion risk having an even more negative effect in abused children that are already much marginalized in the midst of their families. Such measures may dangerously reinforce a feeling of rejection and pupils may be driven to completely disinvest in their school environment to the extent of "dropping out", that is quit school prematurely and therefore without a final certificate (Doudin, 1996; Hébert & Livernoche, 2000). This exposes pupils to important problems of professional and social integration.

However, schools can resort to other measures of help which enable them to utilize teachers' already important efforts and skills while avoiding the negative effects previously mentioned. This requires a fundamental change in perspective. Measures of help generally used (such as support, holding pupils back a year, and parallel classes) are direct interventions focused exclusively on problem-pupils (in which teachers or specialists intervene directly with a child) and neglect teacher-pupil interaction. However, either abused children with learning difficulties or those that adopt behaviors that singularly deteriorate classroom atmosphere (Crittenden, 1993) can become menacing for teachers and other pupils. Teachers then risk feeling particularly powerless and may lose control of the situation. In such difficult situation, at least two people are in need of support. Interventions of an indirect type (in which specialists meet with a teacher instead of a pupil), because of the anonymity they introduce, can constitute an effective support. For example, educational supervision (see Schulte, Osborne & McKinney, 1990; Acheson & Gall, 1992; Saint-Laurent, Giasson, Simard, Dionne & Royer, 1995) gives teachers the opportunity to voice difficulties they face in a meeting with a specialist. By providing feedback on their teaching methods and by analyzing characteristics of their educational relationship with pupils experiencing difficulties, this supervision enables teachers to look at situations differently and to develop optimal teaching strategies. This type of intervention also helps teachers maintain a relational style that allows them to provide children with warm support and positive expectations, and it helps them develop children's sense of belonging to the school community – even under circumstances that are sometimes difficult (see the previously mentioned three factors of compensation defined by Werner & Smith, 1992). Supervision can also keep teachers from engaging in interactions that are physically or psychologically abusive towards pupils, such as rejection.

Furthermore, networking (e.g., Guidoux & Mégroz, 2000) is also an effective means, even a condition of effectiveness, for any intervention, particularly in the academic field (McCulloch & Curonici, 1997). Indeed, teachers cannot and must not make up for deficiencies on their own. When faced with serious neurological, emotional, and cognitive after-effects that can impede abused children's schooling, teachers must actively collaborate with various specialists (Hart, Brassard & Carlson, 1996).

4. An example of intervention

As was mentioned at the beginning of this chapter, the specialized institution in question opted for children's integration in a regular school.

With regard to the learning and behavior difficulties presented by some of these children, and difficulties expressed by teachers in regard to their integration within their class, the headmaster of the specialized institution and the school decided to reinforce the inter-institutional partnership. Thus the position of mediator (a trained teacher) between both institutions was created. This dual institutional affiliation allowed the mediator to intervene directly by offering academic support to the children (at school, during school-time, but outside the classroom), help with homework (in the institution), and intervene indirectly with the children by supervising the school teachers or the educators in the specialized institution.

At the same time, and in the network perspective, a group was formed comprised of the specialized institution's and the school's headmasters, the mediator, a representative of the school's teachers, a representative of the specialized institution's educators, a psychologist, and two researchers involved in the intervention's evaluation. Regular meetings made it possible (1) to define and adjust the roles of the different participants, (2) to recognize problems and conflicts between professionals, and (3) to solve them, or at least control them in order to maintain a work alliance between participants.

Evaluation of the intervention

Evaluation of the effectiveness of the intervention is indispensable for effective management of the school system and allocated financial aid. This evaluation is even more necessary since, as mentioned previously, many forms of school integration assistance have disappointing effects, indeed contrary to those expected (Crahay, 1996; Doudin, 1998). Hereafter, we briefly expound the evaluation method.

The intervention concerns children ($n=26$)[1] aged 7 to 14 years, subjected to various forms of abuse in their families and placed in a specialized institution (boarding school). To recognize possible consequences of abuse on the children's development, we compared them to a group of children ($n=26$) that were not abused.

First, to identify risk factors, a questionnaire was developed to collect data on each abused child and his family history. Then, in order to evaluate consequences of risk factors on the children's development and school integration, and to identify possible effects of compensation factors proper to the school and the teacher, on three occasions (at the beginning of the mediator's intervention, then two and three years after the beginning of her intervention), each child answered seven scales comprised of approximately fifteen questions each. These seven scales were constructed from the works of Grisay (1997), Meuret and Marivain (1997), and Williams and Batten (1981). Two scales investigated the *metacognitive* dimension: management of schoolwork (learning strategies, doing homework); activity *versus* passivity with regard to schoolwork. Three scales investigated the *conative* dimension: image of self in a school context (scholastic and social abilities), motivation; feeling of control in school situations (attributive style, propensity to collaborate *versus* compete); projection into the future (relative to schooling and professional insertion). Two scales investigated the socio-affective dimension: relationship (with teachers and peers); feelings (toward school and life). Finally, we compared the abused children's retention and promotion rates and class setting at the end of each school year (held back a year or placed in a class for pupils with difficulties).

Each time information was collected (beginning, middle, and end of intervention), the statistical analyses focused on comparing abused children to children that were not abused, with regard to (1) their overall scores on each scale and (2) their answers to each item on the scales. Moreover, in order to better apprehend the children's development between the beginning and the end of the intervention, statistical analyses focused on comparing each group of children with regard to (3) overall scores on each scale at the time of the first and third data collections.

Characteristics of abused children

The majority of abused children (18/26) came from three or four different educational contexts (family of origin, foster home, specialized institution). Likewise, a majority of children (16/26) frequented three or four different schools.

With regard to family structure (see table 1), the conjugal link between biological parents of abused children was broken in 25 of 26 cases. Cases of divorce between biological parents were most frequent (16/26). Tragic situations, such as murder (2/26), the suicide of one parent (2/26) or the loss of a brother or sister (3/26) were also noted. Most families were reconstituted (17/26), that is, one of the two parental figures was not the child's biological parent.

Table 1
Characteristics of the family structure of abused children

Characteristics	Children (n=26)
Broken conjugal link between the child's biological parents	25
Cause of the break-up:	
a) Divorce	16
b) Departure or expulsion from Switzerland	2
c) Escape from the country of origin without the spouse	2
d) Murder of one of the parents	2
e) Suicide of one of the parents	2
f) Death of one of the parents without specified cause	1
Death of a sibling	3
Reconstituted family	17

As we can see in table 2, all the children were abused (26/26). They all suffered psychological abuse (26/26) and for the most part also suffered neglect (17/26). A minority suffered physical (5/26) or sexual (3/26) abuse. All of their biological parents were also abused as children (49/49). As in the case of their children, neglect (21/49) and psychological abuse (25/49) were the most frequent. Compared with their own children, proportionally more parents suffered physical abuse (18/49). A similar proportion of parents and children suffered sexual abuse (8/49). Thus, intergenerational transmission of abuse phenomena seems very high in the population studied, primarily concerning neglect and psychological abuse. Furthermore, every pair of biological parents (24/24) was comprised of two adults that were abused as children which seems to reinforce the subsequent risk of abusing their own children. On the other hand, to our knowledge, in cases of remarriage and in a clear majority of cases (16/22), the new spouse was not abused as a child.

Table 2
Frequency of abuse suffered by children, their biological parents or stepparents when they were children, according to type (possibility of several answers per subject)

Types of abuse	Children ($n=26$)	Fathers and/or mothers ($n=49$)	Stepmothers and/or stepfathers ($n=22$)
All types of abuse	26	49	6
Neglect	17	21	6
Psychological abuse	26	25	0
Physical abuse	5	18	1
Sexual abuse	3	8	0

Socio-professional integration of biological parents at the time their child was placed in a specialized institution (table 3) was precarious in several cases. For example, parents that worked full-time or part-time constituted a minority (20/49). Some parents were incarcerated (3/49), deceased (5/49) or received public assistance (6/49) or disablement insurance (3/49). In the reconstituted families, the situation of stepmothers and, more markedly, that of stepfathers was also precarious. For example, barely more than half of them worked (13/22).

Table 3
Socio-professional situation of parents or stepparents at the time the child was placed in a specialized institution

Socio-professional situation	Mothers ($n=26$)	Fathers ($n=23$)	Stepmothers ($n=11$)	Stepfathers ($n=11$)
Full-time work	4	7	5	4
Part-time work	6	3	4	0
Unemployment	0	4	0	4
Public assistance	5	1	0	1
Disablement insurance	1	2	1	1
Housewife	8	-	0	-
Incarcerated	1	2	0	0
Deceased	1	4	0	0
Status unknown	2	-	1	1

The parents' health was also problematic (table 4). There were several cases of hospitalization or ambulatory treatments for physical (6/49) and mostly psychological (49/49) illnesses and addictions – alcohol, drugs, medication (29/49). In reconstituted families, proportionally, stepfathers' situations were just as precarious as that of the fathers. On the other hand, stepmothers seemed in relatively good health. In cases of remarriage, women seemed to have a greater tendency than men to choose a new symptomatic spouse.

Table 4
State of health of parents and stepparents (possibility of several answers per subject)

State of health	Mothers (n=26)	Fathers (n=23)	Stepmothers (n=11)	Stepfathers (n=11)
Hospitalization for physical illness	4	2	0	2
Hospitalization for psychological illness	7	13	0	3
Incarceration	1	8	0	2
Alcohol dependence	6	5	0	2
Drug addiction	3	3	0	-
Medication dependence	8	4	0	1
Psychotherapeutic ambulatory treatment	19	11	0	3

In table 5, we see that some of the children manifested violent behavior prior to or during their placement in an institution. Serious verbal attacks (e.g., insults) were the most frequent prior to placement (12/26) and during placement (14/26). Physical attacks against others were more frequent before placement (7/26) than during placement (4/26); likewise, attacks against other people's property (theft, vandalism, etc.) were more frequent prior to placement (7/26) than during placement (3/26).

Table 5
Violent behavior manifested by children prior to and during placement in the institution (possibility of several answers per subject)

Types of violent behavior	Prior to placement ($n=26$)	During placement ($n=26$)
Physical attacks against others	7	4
Attacks against others' property	7	3
Verbal attacks against others	12	14

5. Results of the intervention

At the beginning of the intervention, there were no significant statistical differences between the two populations (abused children and children which were not abused) regarding overall scores in 6 out of 7 scales. More specifically, we note that nothing distinguished both populations on the socio-affective scale which tested quality of relationship with teachers: thus, both groups of children manifested positive feelings towards their teachers (feelings of being heard, helped, treated fairly, respected.). This is an important result with regard to factors of compensation, and we will come back to it in our discussion of the results of the intervention. Nevertheless, the two populations differed on the meta-cognitive scale testing "management of schoolwork": abused children obtained a significantly lower result than children that were not abused regarding their aptitude for schoolwork management. A detailed analysis, item per item, in each scale showed differences between groups. The meta-cognitive scale investigating management of schoolwork revealed that when abused children find it difficult to follow a lesson in class, they showed a greater tendency than children that have not been abused to "stop listening since it's no use" and to "think of something else"; likewise, they showed a greater tendency to have trouble "finishing schoolwork during the time allocated in class." On the conative scale, investigating the feeling of control in school situations, the two populations differed in their attributive style: abused children tended to attribute the causes of their failure to internal factors and the causes of their success to external factors, whereas children that have not been abused tended to attribute their failures to external causes and their successes to internal causes. On the socio-affective scale concerning feelings towards school and life, abused children showed a greater tendency than children that were not abused to not consider school as "a place where they feel good." This overall negative feeling towards the school seems to contradict the generally positive feelings of relationships with their teachers previously mentioned. Another overall feeling also enables us to distinguish both populations: the abused children showed a greater tendency to "be dissatisfied with their life."

Results from during the intervention did not show a significant statistical difference between both populations with regard to their overall scores in the seven scales. An item per item analysis in each scale showed that in the conative scale, investigating the feeling of control in school situations, we found the same differences between populations in regard to their attributive style as in the first data collection. However, on the socio-affective scale that relates to feelings towards school and life, there was no longer a difference between populations with regard to the overall feeling towards the school and their own life; feelings of abused children towards school and their life in general improved. Two other differences on this scale appeared in this second data collection, whereas, they did not appear in the first: abused children manifested a desire to collaborate with other pupils in class more frequently than children that have not been abused; likewise, abused children were generally more satisfied regarding their relations with classmates than children that have not been abused.

At the end of the intervention, results did not show a difference between the two populations in the seven scales' overall scores. An item by item analysis showed that on the conative scale investigating feelings of control in school situations there was no longer a difference between the two populations with regard to their attributive style. Both populations tended to attribute their failures to external causes, and their successes to internal causes. On the socio-affective scale concerning quality of relations, as during the second data collection, abused children manifested a desire to collaborate with other pupils in class more frequently than do children that have not been abused, likewise, abused children were generally more satisfied with their relations with classmates than children that have not been abused. A new difference appeared during this third collection of data on the scale testing the meta-cognitive dimension: when they did not understand, abused children tended to "ask their teacher for additional explanations" more than children that have not been abused.

Comparison of each of the two groups of children with regard to their overall score on the different scales during the first and third collection of data (beginning and end of the intervention) showed that at the end of the intervention abused children had a superior score in the conative scale investigating projection into the future in regard to schooling and professional insertion. They made more professional plans, they more frequently wished to pursue their studies, and they were more optimistic about their future. On the other hand, we noted no difference in children that have not been abused; they did not evolve during the same lapse of time.

The proportion of abused children placed in classes for children with difficulties, because they were considered incapable of following a regular class, decreased during the intervention. In the year prior to the intervention, 8/26 abused children were in classes for children with difficulties, whereas there were 5/26 at the end of the project. The same applied for the proportion of pupils held back a year: 12/26 abused children were held back during the year prior to the intervention, whereas in the last year taken into account, no child was held back.

6. Conclusions

These children's life stories confirm results from studies on abused children and their families by showing the chaotic aspects of these children's environment. To the abuse they have suffered were added factors that impeded children's optimal development, such as: relational break-ups generated by frequent changes in educational and academic contexts, divorce of parents, hospitalization or incarceration of a parent or death of a family member. Parents' physical and mental health together with difficulties regarding socio-professional integration jeopardized their parental responsibility, commitment, and their children's construction of reference and support points. Furthermore, high risk of intergenerational transmission and maltreatment was also confirmed: without exception, abusive parents were abused as children and, in some cases; their children also came to adopt abusive behavior.

The small difference between abused children and children that have not been abused noted during the first data collection, with regard to overall scores in the different scales and each of their items, lead us to suppose that much work was realized by the school's and specialized institution's professionals prior to our setting up the intervention. Additionally, the different positive feelings manifested by the abused children toward their teachers (feelings of being heard, helped, treated fairly, and respected) may indicate that the three compensation factors previously mentioned (warm support relationships, positive expectations on the part of adults and a sense of belonging to a community) were already effectively provided by the school.

However, the intervention made it possible to improve the school situation and made the school's action even more coherent with regard to compensation factors. As such, the intervention appeared to have enabled the abused children to progress in their management of schoolwork and to better project themselves toward a professional future. The desire to collaborate with their classmates increased and they turned to their teacher more often in cases of learning difficulties. Their overall negative feeling in relation to school disappeared which contradicted generally positive feelings in their relationship with their teacher. For a majority of children, being held back a year and being sent outside regular classes were measures that may lead to an opposite effect (decrease in self-esteem and in learning motivation, school marginalization) as these go against the feeling of belonging to the school community (Doudin, 1996). Resorting to holding pupils back a year has now been eradicated and sending pupils outside the regular class has diminished.

In conclusion, the intervention made it possible to reach the objective pursued, namely the improvement of quality of school integration. Risk factors linked to the family context were established and positive effects resulting from compensation factors were also identified in the educational context and reinforced by the intervention. As mentioned at the beginning of this chapter, successful school integration represents an important organizing factor of development (Cicchetti, Toth & Hennessy, 1993). Results of this intervention allow us to be more optimistic about the future of abused children in relation to their socio-professional insertion and their integration of a positive identification model through the quality of teacher-pupil interactions, the later being an essential condition to impede intergenerational transmission of violence.

References

Acheson, K.A., & Gall, M.D. (1992). *Techniques in the clinical supervision of teachers*. New York: Longman.

Belsky, J. (1980). Child maltreatment: An ecological integration. *American Psychologist, 3*, 320-325.

Christoffel, K.K., Schiedt, P.F., Agran, J.F., Kraus, J.F., McLoughlin, E., & Paulson, J.A. (1992). Standard definitions for childhood injury research: Excerpts of a conference report. *Pediatrics, 89*(6), 1027-1034.

Cicchetti, D., & Rizley, R. (1981). Developmental perspectives on the etiology, intergenerational transmission, and sequelae of child maltreatment. *New Directions for Child Maltreatment, 11*, 31-55.

Cicchetti, D., Toth, S.L., & Hennessy, K. (1993). Child maltreatment and school adaptation: Problems and promises. In D. Cicchetti & S.L. Toth (Eds.), *Child Abuse, Child Development and Social Policy. Advances in Applied Developmental Psychology* (pp. 301-330). Norwood, NJ: Ablex Publishing Company.

Crahay, M. (1996). *Peut-on lutter contre l'échec scolaire?* Brussels: De Boeck.

Crittenden, P.M. (1993). An information-processing perspective on the behavior of neglectful parents. *Criminal Justice and Behavior, 20*(1), 27-48.

Cyrulnik, B. (1999). *Un merveilleux malheur*. Paris: Odile Jacob.

Doudin, P.-A. (1996). Élèves en difficultés: la pédagogie compensatoire est-elle efficace? *Psychoscope, 17*(9), 4-7.

Doudin, P.-A. (1998). *La situation scolaire des élèves étrangers dans l'enseignement vaudois : l'exemple des élèves portugais*. Berne: CDIP/EDK.

Doudin, P.-A., & Erkohen-Marküs, M. (Eds.) (2000). *Violences à l'école: fatalité ou défi?* Brussels: De Boeck.

Egeland, B., & Susman-Stillman, A. (1996). Dissociation as a mediator of child abuse across generations. *Child Abuse and Neglect, 20*(11), 1123-1132.

Erkohen-Marküs, M., & Doudin, P.-A. (2000). Le devenir de l'enfant violenté et sa scolarité. In P.-A. Doudin & M. Erkohen-Marküs (Eds.), *Violence à l'école : fatalité ou défi?* (pp. 23-52). Brussels: De Boeck.

Erkohen-Marküs, M., & Doudin, P.-A. (2001a). Enfants abusés: quel rôle pour l'école? In J. Torrente (Ed.), *La maltraitance: regards pluridisciplinaires* (pp. 141-146). Paris: Hommes et Perspectives.

Erkohen-Marküs, M., & Doudin, P.-A. (2001b). Institutions spécialisées: comment échapper à la violence? *Actualités Psychologiques, 9*, 75-85.

Friend, M. (1988). Putting consultation into context: Historical and contemporary perspectives. Remedial and Special Education, 9, 7-13.

Grisay, A. (1997). *Évaluation des acquis cognitifs et socio-affectifs des élèves au cours des années de college*. Paris: Ministère de l'Éducation Nationale de la Recherche et de la Technologie, Direction de l'Évaluation et de la Prospective.

Guidoux, L., & Mégroz, C. (2000). Équipe pluridisciplinaire et travail de réseau. In P.-A. Doudin & M. Erkohen-Marküs (Eds.), *Violence à l'école : fatalité ou défi?* (pp. 305-326). Brussels: De Boeck.

Hart, S.N., Brassard, M.R., & Carlson, H.C. (1996). Psychological maltreatment. In J. Briere, L. Berliner, J.A. Bulkley, C. Jenny & T. Reid (Eds.), *The APSAC handbook on child maltreatment* (pp. 72-89). Thousand Oaks, CA: Sage.

Hébert, J., & Livernoche, J. (2000). Le décrochage scolaire: une forme de violence psychologique. In P.-A. Doudin & M. Erkohen-Marküs (Eds.), *Violence à l'école: fatalité ou défi?* (pp. 189-195). Brussels: De Boeck.

Kaufman, J., & Zigler, E. (1989). The intergenerational transmission of child abuse. In D. Cicchetti & V. Carlson (Eds.), *Child maltreatment: Theory and research on the causes and the consequences of child abuse and neglect* (pp. 129-150). Cambridge, MA: Cambridge University Press.

Lynch, M.A., & Cicchetti, D. (1992). Maltreated children's reports of relatedness to their teachers. *New Directions for Child Development, 57,* 81-107.

McCulloch, P., & Curonici, C. (1997). *Psychologues et enseignants: regards systémiques sur les difficultés scolaires*. Brussels: De Boeck.

Meuret, D., & Marivain T. (1997). *Inégalités de bien-être à l'école*. Paris: Ministère de l'Éducation Nationale de la Recherche et de la Technologie, Direction de l'Évaluation et de la Prospective.

Mingat, A. (1991). Les activités de rééducation GAPP à l'école primaire. Analyse du fonctionnement et évaluation des effets. *Revue française de sociologie, 32,* 515-549.

Pons, F., Doudin, P.-A., Harris P.L., & de Rosnay, M. (2002). Métaémotion et intégration scolaire. In L. Lafortune & P. Mongeau (Eds.), *L'affectivité dans l'apprentissage* (pp. 7-28). Québec: Presses de l'Université du Québec.

Pons, F., Harris, P.L., & Doudin, P.-A. (2002). Teaching emotion understanding. *European Journal of Psychology of Education, 17*(3), 293-304.

Rutter, M. (1989). Psychosocial resilience and protective mechanisms. In D. Cicchetti & V. Carlson (Eds.), *Child Maltreatment: Theory and Research On The Causes and Consequences of Child Abuse and Neglect* (pp. 181-214). New York: Cambridge University Press.

Saint-Laurent, L., Giasson, J., Simard, C., Dionne, J., & Royer, E. (Eds.) (1995). *Programme d'intervention auprès des élèves à risques : une nouvelle option educative*. Montreal: Gaëtan Morin.

Schulte, A.C., Osborne, S.S., & McKinney, J.D. (1990). Academic outcomes for students with learning disabilities in consultation and resource programs. *Exceptional Children, 57,* 162-172.

Seligman, M.E.P. (1991). *Learned Optimism.* New York: Knopf.
Werner, E. E., & Smith, R. (1992). *Vulnerable but invincible: A longitudinal study of resilient children and youth. New York:* Adams, Bannister & Cox.
Will, M.L. (1986). Educating children with learning problems: A shared responsibility, *Exceptional Children, 52,* 411-415.
Williams, T., & Batten, M. (1981). *The quality of school life.* Hawthorn (Victoria): Australian Council for Educational Research Monograph, Vol. 12.

---

[1] Each abused child was coupled with a same sex child that was not abused, in the same grade and the same class (paired sampling).

CHAPTER 3

Learning to philosophize in preschool: A step toward primary prevention of violence?

Marie-France Daniel, Emmanuelle Auriac-Peyronnet, and Michael Schleifer

1. Introduction

Too often, in our society, the body is dissociated from the person. It is industrialized, exploited, or even abused. In this regard, a few years ago, the Ministère de la Sécurité publique du Québec registered 3,202 violent criminal offenses against children aged 0 to 12 (MSQ, 1999). Studies indicate that before reaching the age of maturity, one out of three women and one out of six men will be victims of sexual assault (Tourigny & Guillot, 1999). The Canadian Centre for Justice suggests that 67% of victims are assaulted in their homes, 17% in public areas, and 16.25% in public institutions and establishments. The Association des centres jeunesse du Québec reports that in 2001, nearly 6,000 youngsters were referred for behavioral problems and nearly 6,500 for sexual or physical mistreatment (Paré, 2002). On an academic level, violence has a negative impact on the child victim. Among the behaviors observed are a lack of intellectual appetence, memorization problems, attention disorders, learning difficulties, low self-esteem, and other behavioral problems such as aggression, isolation, and extreme dependence upon the teacher (Erkohen-Markus & Doudin, 2000). Generally speaking, confusion and silence characterize children who are victims of abuse. They do not understand what is happening to them. The causes elude them completely, and often they convince themselves of their own responsibility with regard to the other person's violent behavior. Moreover, they are unable to communicate what they are experiencing. Children who are victims of violence and children who are aggressors have characteristics in common: lack of self-esteem, non-critical judgment, and difficulty communicating, particularly their emotions.

In the following pages, we present: (1) philosophical support in connection with the body and violence prevention; and (2) the effects of philosophical intervention among pre-school children on the development of their dialogical competencies and on the modification of their representations of four basic emotions (i.e., happiness, sadness, anger, and fear).

There are three levels of prevention: primary, secondary, and tertiary. We concentrate on "primary" prevention – that which is intended for a healthy population and is directed toward anticipating the ill effects of violence. Authors who hold the theory that schools can participate in this type of prevention imply that interventions should begin from the elementary level (i.e., from the age of six or seven) (in particular, see Lapointe et al., 1993, 1996; Nafpaktitis et al., 1998). Other works have shown that young children are capable of reflecting on their emotions so as to understand their causes and consequences, and that this reflection tends to regulate their social interactions (Harris & Pons, 2003). Given that violent behaviors appear very early in children (Dodson, 1972; Dumas, 2000), our position is that children should begin reflection and dialogue on emotions and manifestations of violence as early as pre-school (i.e., from the age of five).

2. Philosophical material in connection with the body and prevention of violence

The Philosophy for Children (P4C) approach, conceived by Matthew Lipman and colleagues at Montclair State University (Lipman, Sharp & Oscanyan, 1980) appears to be a relevant educational paradigm for participation in primary prevention of violence among children[1]. Several studies show that regular (one hour per week) and sustained (throughout a school year) use of P4C has positive impacts on the development of youngsters' critical thinking. In addition, it fosters their capacity to engage in an authentic dialogue with their peers (in particular, see: Daniel, Lafortune, Pallascio & Schleifer, 2000).

Lipman's material is intended for children aged 6 to 15 and is inspired by fields of philosophy – logic, metaphysics, ethics and aesthetics. Due to lack of relevant material explicitly aimed at violence prevention and intended for pre-school children, *The Tales of Audrey-Anne* (Daniel, 2002a), was developed. The work is a collection of 16 philosophical tales that question "open" concepts for which there are no single answers, and upon which the children are invited to reflect as a group. The tales highlight concepts inherent in manifestations of violence, in the person, the body, intimacy, identity, rights, etc. The objectives of this philosophical support are the stimulation of social and dialogical competencies in pre-school children, as well as awareness of their body, consciousness of various manifestations of violence (physical, verbal, sexual), and development of cognitive skills.

Are five and six-year-old children capable of "philosophizing"? In other words, are they capable of reflecting in a constructivist manner and of dialoguing with peers? Experimentation in France and in Quebec using the *Tales of Audrey-Anne* clearly illustrates the capacity of children aged four to six to philosophize on concepts related to the body and to manifestations of violence (Daniel, 2002b; Daniel & Michel, 2001). A teacher's guide (Daniel, 2003) was also written to assist teachers with their philosophical facilitation. This work comprises more than 300 discussion plans and exercises that correspond to the content of each tale.

Each of the 16 tales develops with regard to three dimensions. The first dimension is related to body and emotions. It includes discussion plans and exercises linked to games, private and public parts of the body, the five senses, mobility, spatial orientation, and relaxation, and to emotions, such as anger, fear, happiness, sadness, shame, and surprise. The second dimension of *The Tales of Audrey-Anne* presents situations (generally more implicit than explicit) that can lead the children, if the situations interest them, to question manifestations of physical violence (a butterfly with a torn wing, a doll whose hair has been pulled out, etc.), sexual violence (a ladybug that tries to charm another into showing its bottom, etc.), and psychological violence (having fun scaring a puppy, saying words that make another person feel ridiculous, etc.). The third dimension that appears in each of *The Tales of Audrey-Anne* is related to cognitive development (questioning, observing, exploring, organizing, placing in a hierarchy, comparing, making analogies, justifying one's opinions, elaborating on hypotheses, inventing games, predicting consequences, distinguishing between intentions and consequences, establishing relationships between parts and a whole, criticizing, etc.), which is actualized through discussion plans and exercises. With regard to emotional and social development, this occurs through regular (one hour per week) and sustained (throughout the school year) use of the P4C approach itself, which is centered on philosophical dialogue within a "community of inquiry."

3. Some pedagogical tips

The method used to make the most of the Audrey-Anne philosophical material is suggested by the P4C approach: (1) the teacher reads a tale to the children; (2) the children are then invited to ask philosophical questions triggered by the reading and which they would like to discuss as a group; and (3) together, the children attempt to answer the question they chose and, in order to do so, they conduct a philosophical dialogue. Bellow are a few educational leads relating to each step.

Reading the tales

First, it should be noted that *The Tales of Audrey-Anne* deliberately contains few illustrations. Those that are included are marked by sobriety so as to give children all the space necessary to imagine each character and their experiences in whichever way is most meaningful to them.

Because five-year-old children generally do not read, the reading is left to the teacher. This can either be done in the traditional manner or can take the form of a puppet show, which children particularly appreciate. Six-year-old children usually appreciate reading the tales themselves with the children reading aloud and in turn (one sentence per child). These two elements are important to mark "cooperation" among peers. Indeed, sometimes shy children only express themselves when reading (they either do not or hardly participate in the following stages of the approach). This first step toward sharing ideas develops gradually as philosophical practices take place.

In choosing the tales, it is preferable to respect the order in which they are presented because the problems increase in complexity. Thus, in a first group of tales, emphasis is placed on manifestations of physical violence (e.g., a large butterfly has torn the wing of a small one; Jane pulled Audrey-Anne's doll's hair out, etc.). A second group of tales focuses on manifestations of sexual violence (e.g., a ladybug wants another ladybug to take off its underwear; a baby-sitter holds Nick too long in his arms, etc.). A third group demonstrates concepts related to verbal and psychological violence (e.g., children have fun terrorizing a puppy; a gang of older kids making fun of Vincent, etc.). Finally, the last tale deals with social violence (Bernice is poor and she is different from the other kids).

Collecting questions

After reading the tale, the children are invited to ask questions. This second step presupposes that the children have put enough effort into comprehending the tale that they are concerned about the situations described. Comprehension does not only require knowledge of words, but also global understanding of context. This step encourages the children to enter a process of inquiry which is the basis for any well thought-out judgment.

Learning to ask questions is difficult, yet learning to do so is fundamental in that it leads one to surpass personal opinions, prejudices, and experiences. Furthermore, the second step gives responsibility to the children and places them at the forefront of their learning because through their questions, children (rather than adults) determine the discussion agenda. Therefore, collecting questions ensures philosophical sessions that are rooted in intrinsic motivation. It should be noted that the teacher can, during a one-hour session, cover all of the children's questions or choose to explore a single one in-depth. At the beginning of the school year, we recommend dealing with many questions to cognitively stimulate children. The teacher can then adjust to the children's capacity for reflection according to their progress with philosophical practice. The second step presupposes that the children learn to formulate not only a question, but a "philosophical" question. To this day, experimentation with *The Tales of Audrey-Anne* has shown that, from the age of five, children are capable of formulating this type of question if they are guided by a teacher. Thus, during the first weeks, after reading a tale, the teacher asks the children to state what they liked or what they remember from the tale. The children then formulate comments rather than questions: "Vincent wanted to put his hand on Audrey-Anne's bottom."

Once the children have understood this process, the teacher suggests they begin their sentence with "Why...?" or with "Does...?" Gradually, the teacher adds a third term to their vocabulary: "What does ... mean?", and so on. In a general manner, we can say that a child's question carries a philosophical meaning when it:

- Concerns "why" rather than "how";
- Questions concepts (e.g., "What is ...?" and "What does ... mean?");
- Develops around the origin, cause, consequences, relationships (logical and linguistic) between words, concepts, or ideas (e.g., "Where does ... come from?" and "What will happen if ...?");
- Questions experiences, traditions, prejudices (e.g., "Is it true that ...?" and "Why do we think that ...?");
- Searches for justifications of peers' statements (e.g., "Why do you say that?").

When collecting questions, the teacher notes children's comments or questions on the blackboard (with words or pictograms) exactly as they are formulated. She adds the child's name to identify the "owner." This is the concrete sign that the child is part of the community of inquiry.

Philosophical dialogue among peers

A dialogue is said to be philosophical when the children, instead of lingering over personal anecdotes, search for the meaning of concepts, question, give their opinion, justify this opinion with sound reasons, find similarities and differences, offer counter-examples, work out relationships between concepts, are critical towards the statements of others, and self-correct. Indeed, the objective of the exchanges is not for the children to recount personal situations in relation to manifestations of violence, but rather to encourage them to reflect upon concepts related to these situations. For example, take a situation in which a child realizes a friend has torn the child's drawing. Some approaches suggest verbalization ("My friend made me unhappy when he tore my drawing") and thus turn the child's attention (*intra*-subjectively) to the unhappiness of "I" caused by "you" or "him." In a different and complementary manner, the philosophical approach suggests helping the child reflect (*inter*-subjectively) upon concepts inherent in the situation. Here are a few examples of questions that could be asked of the children:

- What is a friend?
- Is it easy to be someone's friend? Why?
- Is it possible to fight with a friend? Why?
- Is tearing a friend's drawing a violent gesture?
- Is it more or less violent than tearing a tissue paper? Why?
- What is sadness? What is anger?
- What are the similarities and differences between anger and sadness?

Thus, as their philosophical (conceptual) reflection progresses, the children understand not only the action that is at stake, but also the ins and outs of it. In so doing, they begin to comprehend the world that surrounds them and acquire the tools to control it rather than being simply subjected to it. It should be pointed out that the objective of the third step is not for the children to argue in a competitive manner, but to foster dialogue in a perspective of cooperation as each child's intervention contributes to the enrichment of the group's perspective. A true "community of inquiry" is manifested when dialogue among peers is marked by respect, open-mindedness, and tolerance.

Following a philosophical intervention among five-year-old children which took place over a school year (October to April)[2], we attempted to answer these two questions: Are five-year-old children capable of conducting a dialogue among peers? Does learning to dialogue have an effect on the representations these children have of four basic emotions (happiness, fear, anger and sadness)? In the following sections, we present an analysis of transcripts from the children's exchanges, as well as results concerning their representations of emotions.

4. Learning to "dialogue" among peers with *The Tales of Audrey-Anne*

At first, the research project's objective was to establish to what extent five-year-old children could, with philosophical support, improve their cognitive and dialogical competences. Analysis of the first transcript indicates that, at the beginning of the experiment, the children are not able to formulate a question from a tale. They express themselves with one or two words only. They do not speak to each other but are satisfied with responding to the teacher. The exchange lasts only 10 minutes, after which the children lose concentration and motivation. Only two or three children express themselves while the majority listens in silence. Even when stimulated, they are not able to justify their opinions. The cognitive acts that characterized their speech are simple (statements and personal examples).

Another transcript was analyzed at the conclusion of the experiment six months later. In this section, we present an analysis of a few excerpts from this exchange[3]. In accordance with the P4C approach, after reading the tale entitled *Philip's Father* (see Appendix), the children were invited to formulate their questions. Here are a few examples:

A: What is your question?
70: Why did Philip wear a [hearing] aid on his ears?
76: Why was he (Philip) crying?
77: Why (...) did Audrey-Anne place herself behind the shoes?
69: Was he playing hide-and-seek (...) in the closet?
68: Why does Philip have hearing aids?
75: [Why did Philip's father] say bad words?

Here we note that several children adequately formulate questions related to the tale's secondary and principal ideas. Questions are neither conceptual nor philosophical, but they are *not* a matter of simple text comprehension. Indeed, the answers are not to be found within the tale. On the contrary, these questions are bearers of discussions for the children.

A: So I would like [to start with] the first question: Why did Philip have a hearing aid?
71: Because he wanted to hear (...)
70: If he didn't wear one, people would yell and he wouldn't hear anything. They would yell and Philip wouldn't like that.

In this excerpt, in relation to the first question, two children express themselves and complement one another. They are both able to identify with the handicapped child and with his surroundings. On the one hand, 71 states Philip's perspective (he wants to hear). On the other hand, 70 establishes a sequence of causal relationships. First, a direct consequence is established that stems from reasoning (If he didn't wear one, he wouldn't hear anything) and not from direct sensorial experience. Then, a hypothetical consequence is established related to the latter (people would yell). Finally, another hypothetical consequence is established related to emotions (Philip wouldn't like that). Thus, logical thinking, which marks coherence and causal relationships, is manifest, as is empathy regarding attitudes.

A:	(…) Now, in the second question, we ask why Philip was crying. 70 said the daddy should comfort the little boy and we would like to know why.
77:	I think that it's children that comfort daddies that are sad sometimes.
75:	In real life, it's the daddy that should have comforted the boy.
A:	Why?
75:	Because if the boy is sad, it's the daddy that has to comfort him.
A:	Do you know why?
70:	Because the boy is too little.
69:	Because a child is more sensitive than an adult.
A:	How is that?
69:	Because a child is smaller and an adult is bigger.
75:	A baby is much more fragile than a child.
A:	Why?
75:	Because it's smaller.
77:	A baby when you hold it, sometimes it can fall.
69:	An adult is heavier than a child … because an adult is stronger and a child is less strong.

In this excerpt, several children unite around the same question. They do not simply answer the facilitator's questions. They are engaged in a process of inquiry where peer points of view serve to enrich the group's perspective. Moreover, the facilitator's contribution is minimal in this excerpt where the children speak with little prompting. Their reflexive and discursive involvement is motivated by a common question. Some children are critical towards the remarks of their peers. Thus, 77 states a point of view that differs from 70's, and 75 reverses 77's proposition, going back to 70's statement but specifying a distinction between the story and "real life." Furthermore, inasmuch as the facilitator stimulates them in this direction, the children justify their points of view ("because the boy is sad;" "because a child is smaller;" "because when you hold it sometimes it can fall."). In their justification process, various comparisons between the adult and the child are established by the children (smaller and bigger; more sensitive; heavier and stronger). If size and strength are a matter of sensorial experience and concrete observation, "sensitivity" is a matter of reasoning and intuitive comprehension of the distinction between adults and children. With respect to comparisons, 75 adds another element that enriches the child-and-adult hierarchy – babies. 75 does not take up the preceding characteristics, but adds another (fragility) that he appropriately justifies. His justification is completed by 77 who illustrates fragility with an example ("a baby, when you hold it, sometimes it can fall").

A: In the story, why was Philip crying?
76: Because he was sad that his daddy said bad words to him.
74: He was crying because his daddy said a bad word to him.
77: And also, when a daddy says bad words, a child cries. It's better to say nice things.

In this last excerpt, 76 and 74 answer the question. 77 synthesizes both previous interventions by generalizing the remarks. He presents his intervention as a logical rule where the consequence is inevitable and not dissociable from the action ("when a daddy says bad words, a child cries"). He concludes by stating rule of a social and moral order ("it's better to say nice things"). This intervention denotes cognitive skills related to a capacity to abstract, to generalize, and to categorize.

In short, this last exchange indicates that, as the weeks go by, the children, in spite of a certain epistemological egocentricity which is characteristic of this age group, have moved from anecdotal to dialogical exchanges. Indeed, the children asked several questions which were all directly related to the tale. Most children share points of view according to a question formulated by one peer, but discussed by the group. The children listen to each other and build their interventions on their peers' points of view. Higher-order thinking skills and attitudes were used by the children: listening and understanding peer points of view, comparing, establishing consequences and logical relations, placing a series of elements in a hierarchy, providing differing ideas, categorizing specific actions into rules, etc. The thinking modes associated with these skills and attitudes are: logical, creative, meta-cognitive and responsible. Thus, the children evidently developed some cognitive and dialogical competencies.

5. Children's representations of emotions

Within the framework of the same research project, in order to identify and understand the children's representations of four basic emotions (happiness, sadness, anger and fear), we conducted individual interviews with children from groups experimenting with *The Tales of Audrey-Anne* during a school year (experimental groups) and with children from groups that did not have this philosophical support (control groups). The interviews were conducted at the beginning and at the end of the school year (before and after philosophical intervention, in the case of the experimental groups). Analysis of the children's answers brought to light three categories, which were placed in a hierarchy:

(1) Non-represented emotion (e.g., "I don't know what happiness means");
(2) Concretely or egocentrically represented emotion (e.g., "Happiness is when I eat cake");
(3) Socially represented emotion (e.g., "Happiness is playing with my friends.").

During the school year, the children in all groups (experimental and control) modified their representations of emotions, but progress was most marked in the children who benefited from philosophical support. Indeed, at the beginning of the school year, the children were all situated in categories 1 and 2. By the end of the school year, children from the control group were situated in category 2 (concrete representation), while children from the experimental groups were situated in categories 2 and 3 (concrete representation + social representation). Representations of children who used *The Tales of Audrey-Anne* as a starting point for their dialogues were thus marked by a social perspective, which was not characteristic of the other children's representations.

At the end of the philosophical intervention with *The Tales of Audrey-Anne*, the third category, or "social" representation of emotions, was manifested for each of the four emotions as follows. As to happiness, several children now associate it with an interpersonal relationship (e.g., "Happiness is having fun with others"). Thus, thanks to philosophical intervention, a fair number of children have established to a certain degree of awareness that happiness occurs as long as others are present and that it requires personal involvement or active construction of the social relationship rather than simply being subjected to it. These same children developed a socializing representation of anger (e.g., "anger is when you say things that are not very nice" or "it's when someone hits me"). Thus, for the children who benefited from philosophical support during a school year, anger is, from now on, related to a cause, which places interpersonal relations at the forefront. With regard to fear, at the end of the philosophical intervention, children in the experimental groups represented it with real causes (e.g., "fear is when there are noises I don't know") versus imaginary causes, as was the case at the beginning of the year (e.g., "fear is when monsters want to eat me"). Thus, several of them seem not only to better understand the meaning of fear, but also seem to have better control over it, which lets us presuppose that they probably acquired greater confidence in themselves and in the world that surrounds them. Finally, with regard to sadness, the social dimension is manifested in recognizing the contribution of others as a cause of sadness (e.g., "sadness is when you're all alone", "sadness is when my father died"). Not only do these groups of children explicitly represent sadness, but its representations indicate that it is often suffered.

In short, we have noted that the children's representations of four basic emotions can be modified within one school year, and that these representations can acquire a socializing aspect, even at the age of five or six years.

6. Conclusions

Did philosophical practice with the help of *The Tales of Audrey-Anne* contribute to the evolution of children's representations of emotions? Maturity, resulting from the experience of a first year at school in a large group (versus at home or in day-care) and from the transition from age five to age six, played a role. However, if we compare results of analysis from children in the control groups with those from the experimental groups, we can consider that the social and cognitive competencies, constructed through philosophical exchanges among peers during the school year, seem to have a positive impact on the refinement of emotion representation in children, and in particular on the category called "social representation." This is because *The Tales of Audrey-Anne*'s philosophical material aids the global development of the child. In other words, it aims to develop the sensory-motor, cognitive, emotional, and social levels. Thus, several of the philosophical guide's discussion plans and exercises are based on cooperative games and physical activities (sensorimotor level). Furthermore, it suggests discussion plans and exercises to help children know themselves and their strengths and limits, and to better accept themselves as different beings in perpetual evolution (emotional level). However, this material is based on stimulating the cognitive and social levels. As such, the tales suggest everyday situations to the children, but of a conflicting and ambiguous nature. Therefore, they are not easily solved individually. Help from the "community of inquiry" becomes a valued support where each person can express ideas that enrich the group and contribute to improvement of quality of life. Moreover, the Audrey-Anne material does not provide any "right answers" the children must memorize or "proper behavior" they must integrate. It is the children, as a group, who search for elements of response, construct tools, develop strategies, specify processes, choose relationships, criticize ideas, and suggest various contexts so as to resolve meaningful problems in an autonomous, empathic, and critical manner. Several studies have shown that the philosophical community of inquiry fosters elementary school children's predispositions regarding complex thinking, respect for difference and tolerance towards divergent viewpoints (in particular, see Daniel, Lafortune, Pallascio & Schleifer, 2000).

The community of inquiry cannot exist without philosophical dialogue defined by the capability to construct one's own point of view from the statements of peers and by the motivation to enrich one's perspectives from the group's point of view. Thus, children gradually develop their listening skills. Because respect and confidence are prerequisites for dialogue within a community of inquiry, children acquire the self-esteem necessary to express themselves before the group. Complex cognitive skills related to logical, creative, responsible and meta-cognitive thinking are stimulated in children through dialogue (Daniel, Lafortune, Pallascio, Mongeau, Slade, Splitter & De la Garza, in press, 2003).

In summary, practice with philosophical dialogue using *The Tales of Audrey-Anne* as a starting point stimulated the complex thinking skills of the children in the experimental group, as well as their competencies for dialogue with their peers. *A priori*, it also seems to have exerted a positive influence on their representations of emotions, favoring a transition from non-representation to a more socializing representation. However, to confirm this notion, we would have to pursue our interventions in pre-school classrooms with a greater diversity of groups and instruments.

References

Daniel, M.-F. (1998). *La philosophie et les enfants*. Montreal: Logiques (also published with De Boeck in 1997).

Daniel, M.-F. (2002a). *Les contes d'Audrey-Anne*. Quebec City: Le Loup de Gouttière.

Daniel, M.-F. (2002b). Des expériences en maternelle. *Diotime - L'Agora, 13*, 48-55.

Daniel, M.-F. (2003). *Dialoguer sur le corps et la violence: un pas vers la prévention*. Quebec City: Le Loup de Gouttière.

Daniel, M.-F., Lafortune, L., Pallascio, R., Mongeau, P., Slade, C., Splitter, L., & T. De la Garza (in press, 2003). A developmental process of dialogical critical thinking. *Inquiry: Critical Thinking across the Disciplines,*

Daniel, M.-F., Lafortune, L., Pallascio, R., & Schleifer, M. (2000). Developmental dynamics of a community of philosophical inquiry in an elementary school mathematics classroom. *Thinking, 15*(1), 2-10.

Daniel, M.-F., & Michel, A.-M. (2001). Learning to think and to speak: account of an experiment involving children aged 3 to 5 in France and Quebec. *Thinking, 15*(3), 17-26.

Dodson, F. (1972). *Tout se joue avant 6 ans*. Paris: Robert Laffont.

Dumas, J. (2000). *L'enfant violent – le connaître, l'aider, l'aimer*. Paris: Bayard.

Erkohen-Marküs, M., & Doudin, P.-A. (2000). Le devenir de l'enfant violenté et sa scolarité. In P.-A. Doudin & M. Erkohen-Marküs (Eds.), *Violences à l'école. Fatalité ou défi?* (pp. 17-47). Brussels: De Boeck Université.

Harris, P.L., & Pons, F. (2003). Perspectives actuelles sur le développement de la compréhension des émotions chez l'enfant In J.–M. Colletta and A. Tcherkassof (Eds.), *Les émotions. Cognition, langage et développement* (pp. 209–229). Sprimont (Belgique): Mardaga.

Lapointe, Y, Bowen, F., & Laurendeau, M. C. (1993; 1996). *Habiletés prosociales et prévention de la violence en milieu scolaire: Répertoire d'animation pour la première année.* Montreal: Direction de la santé publique de Montréal Centre.

Lipman, M., Sharp, A.M., & Oscanyan, F.S. (1980). *Philosophy in the classroom.* Philadelphia, PA: Temple University Press.

Ministère de la Sécurité publique du Québec. (1999). *Déclaration uniforme de la criminalité* (DUC11) compilation spéciale.

Nafpaktitis, M., & Perlmutter, B.F. (1998). School-based early mental health intervention with at-risk students. *School Psychology Review, 27*(3), 420-432.

Paré, I. (13-11-2002). Centres jeunesse. Les salles d'urgence de la misère. *Le Devoir*, p.1 and 10.

Tourigny, M., & Guillot, M. L. (1999). *Les agressions sexuelles: STOP. Conséquences entourant la prise en charge par les services sociaux et judiciaires des enfants victimes d'agression sexuelle.* Québec: Government of Quebec. Ministère de la Santé et des Services sociaux.

APPENDIX

Philip's father (Tale)

Audrey-Anne and Philip, her boyfriend, are sitting in the back of the closet. The door is half-open, just enough to let a ray of sunshine in to light up Audrey-Anne's mouth. Audrey-Anne likes to sit behind the boxes and the shoes. She likes the smells of her shoes and her clothes. She is comfortable. These are smells she knows. She feels cozy and safe. The closet is her special place, her hideaway. She is sitting on the floor with her knees under her chin.

Philip wears a hearing aid. He doesn't hear voices very well. He doesn't make out words when they are spoken softly or when they are mumbled.

Audrey-Anne is happy. She thinks: "I really like Philip because he always listens when I talk to him."

Then she turns towards Philip and asks:

"Philip, who do you like best? Your daddy or your mom's boyfriend?"

"My daddy, of course! He's my hero! He's the strongest! He's the best daddy in the world!"

"My daddy, too! He's the nicest daddy in the world! I give him lots of hugs and kisses."

"Me too! Mostly if I haven't been nice to him and I want him to forgive me."

"What things do you do when you are naughty, Philip?"

"I don't know!" answers Philip with a shrug. He seems annoyed.

Audrey-Anne insists. She is curious and surprised to find out that her boyfriend can be naughty.

"Give me an example, Philip, or else I won't believe you."

"Well, sometimes, uh... sometimes when my daddy comes home from work at night and is feeling tired. Well, sometimes he says bad words to me and I cry."

Audrey-Anne doesn't understand:

"But, why do you cry, Philip?"

"I don't know. I really don't know. My daddy is such a nice daddy ... He often buys me all kinds of gifts. He loves me so much! But every time he says bad words to me, my heart starts beating really loudly and I get scared."

"You're afraid of words?" asks Audrey-Anne laughing. You really are silly! A word can't hurt you, Philip! A word is, well it's... it's ... it's just a sound, right?"

"You're right, Audrey-Anne. I really am foolish! But when my daddy yells at me that I'm "dense" because I can't understand, it hurts so much!"

"Is that why you say you're naughty?"

"Well, when I cry like that, it makes my daddy sad. So, to make him feel better, I climb on his knees and I give him a big hug so that he will forgive me."

---

[1] For an explanation of the approach as well as an in-depth analysis of its inherent principles, see Daniel (1997/1998).

[2] This experimentation was made possible by a subsidy from the Social Sciences and Humanities Research Council of Canada (SSHRC) from 2001 to 2004.

[3] For reasons of confidentiality, we have replaced the names of the children with numbers; the letter "A" represents the adult.

CHAPTER 4

Negating emotions is useless, and yet!

François Audigier

> *The heart has its reasons, which reason knows not.*
> *We feel it in a thousand things.*
> PASCAL, PENSÉES

> *If I knew the meaning of the story, I would not need to tell it.*
> MUSIL, THE MAN WITHOUT QUALITIES

> *Life's but a walking shadow, a poor player*
> *That struts and frets his hour upon the stage*
> *And then is heard no more. It is a tale*
> *Told by an idiot, full of sound and fury,*
> *Signifying nothing.*
> SHAKESPEARE, MACBETH

1. Introduction

Emotions, affective dimensions, feelings…? Where are all these more or less strange individual aspects of humans, of pupils, hidden in schools? Schools whose legitimacy, pedestal, and horizon is reason. What to do with these ingredients that so often seem to impede comprehension of academic knowledge? We all know the discourses and constructions that oppose reason to emotion, that declare the first to be universal and therefore alone to be noteworthy, and that reject the second to the specific characteristics of an individual, indeed, and this would show a certain openness to those of the culture. Schools, public schools, schools for everyone should have to leave emotional dimensions aside to dedicate themselves to the activities of the mind. Admittedly, divisions in existing teaching disciplines recognize a few places where emotions and its companions are authorized. But in disciplines said to be intellectual, in particular History, Geography and Citizenship Education, which are in question here, suspicion regarding emotions is enduring. A closer look reveals that this suspicion is ambiguous, whether in official texts or in daily class activities, and denial is far from total; if a *priori* emotions are obstacles, turning them into allies would be preferable. Here, youth is better served. The person, each pupil, each teacher, each of us is not so easily carved into slices. What knowledge differentiates, what science separates and constructs to better identify and study, life reunites and firmly secures. The beautiful title of an issue of Raisons pratiques (1995) on this subject expresses it clearly: *The color of thoughts. Feelings, Emotions, Intentions*. Without emotions thoughts would have no color; nothing but gray, between black and white! In *Wings of Desire*, Wim Wenders films paradise in black and white and the world of humans in color.

Emotions? The term is not easily defined. It is not easily differentiated from moods, feelings, judgments, etc; it calls on all these terms and many others to outline a universe with numerous ramifications. Here we consider emotions in a very large sense to which we will subsequently add a few details. Before doing this, four brief stories observed in the classrooms and a few more general findings on teaching our three disciplines will serve to introduce our subject, more so its ambiguities and fluidity. Firstly, there is very little research in our field that explicitly refers to emotions and its associates; we encounter various aspects of these during our exploration. Secondly, we assemble some sources to better establish the status of emotions while leaving room for differences according to each discipline and according to pupils' ages. Thirdly, once denial of emotion is banned and need for its recognition established, this chapter suggests a few possible orientations to work with pupils, orientations where in part we find our introductory stories.

2. Knowledge at the risk of emotions

Let us begin by visiting some classes where pupils are working on different subjects of History, Geography, and Citizenship Education[1].

Concepts and emotions to relate experience

We are in a 5th grade classroom in a French college (pupils aged 12-13 years); this is a difficult class that is comprised of pupils that show little interest in writing, that are often older than the norm and not very interested in what they are being taught. The History, Geography, and Citizenship Education teacher intends to work on the concept of equality. This teacher participates in an action research whose purpose is to experiment the feasibility of Citizenship Education focused on the law; the objective is to construct legal concepts (Audigier & Lagelée, 1996). On this particular day, equality is the subject. The teacher has been forewarned of the relevance of giving importance to what her pupils already know and she is concerned about involvement in their work. After a brief moment of discussion she asks them to relate, in written form, a situation in which they think equality is in question. After a brief hesitation and a moment of blank page anxiety, the pupils commence. In just a few minutes, they have generated one or two-page short stories in which they relate personally experienced situations of inequality. Their tales, although at times awkward and more or less well structured, all express, with force and sometimes with pain and outrage, emotions linked to feelings of injustice, reject and negation of self or kin. "Equality", now here is a word, a concept that takes on meaning only with a strong emotional dimension. It is also a summons for pupils to express their experiences; this appeals to them because equality and what is at stake mobilize this emotional dimension. At last these pupils, reputed to have an aversion to writing, write with relevance and without reserve, to relate situations affecting them; a relation to the world with its overflow of emotions.

No links to knowledge without judgment

Humanitarian action is preferable to a solitary stroll. This recapitulates a moment of discussion allocated to assessing work completed during the school year in a 6th grade History class in Geneva (pupils aged 11-12 years). Three individuals, symbolic of Geneva, had served as a main thread to the year's History lessons: Calvin, Rousseau, and Dunant. Pupils, when asked to say what interested them most and what they remembered most from these lessons, almost unanimously expressed an attraction for Dunant and limited interest for Rousseau. Dunant's active role, the fact that he achieved something readily assessed as positive, places him much higher in pupils' appreciation than Rousseau who dreams as he walks; no matter the connection between his strolls and places they can identify to this day. Thus expressed by the pupils, such a judgment is reasoned according to their arguments. Almost all of these arguments refer to an emotional appreciation, to what they admire, to emotions they experience when confronted to the misfortunes of war and to their identification with the person who attempted to bring some relief. Far more, but this has yet to be corroborated, emotion present here, which overtakes judgment, also determines interest and appears to prefigure what is memorized. Dunant's story seems better remembered than that of Rousseau. It contains drama and positive action, and in truth it is based on a stronger intrigue than that of Rousseau[2]. No matter the regret discreetly expressed by their teacher, the pupils have made their choice and this choice is based on reasons that largely include affective and emotional dimensions.

Cooling down a subject

Now, let us enter a 3rd grade class in a French college (pupils aged 14-15 years.) The teacher is addressing political institutions of the 5th Republic in a Citizenship Education class. She has also been forewarned of the importance of giving pupils the opportunity to express themselves. With a few questions, she elicits knowledge that is supposed, and if not really known, at least conveyed by media enough for some echoes to linger, on which to base the lesson *per se*. Alas! A great hubbub is raised; pupils have a thousand things to say. Once words are disciplined a little, references abound, not about institutions, but about political staff, those seen on television, about the debates, and the oppositions. Far from the institutions themselves, what counts are the people, opinions, and choices, the words heard and judgments spoken. All of this translates into debates, oppositions, which constitute the story line of political life as perceived by the pupils, at least to begin with. But then, what to do with all of these scattered and diverse remarks in which divergent opinions appear? Is there room in the classroom for what divides society, opinions with their hopelessly intertwined information, knowledge, judgments, appreciation, emotions, etc.? There is a great risk that pupils will give free reign to . . . to what? In short, there is danger and teachers are hardly trained to greet such divergences in their teaching. Then of course there is the program and the end of year exam that, when it includes a question of Citizenship Education, focuses on institutions, and leaves aside what may seem too loaded, too hot.

The outcome is predictable. Soon enough, the teacher puts an end to pupil interventions. The usual organizational chart showing institutions with jurisdictions, elections, members, ministers, etc. is placed on the overhead projector. Pupils, which were so alive and so willing to speak during the previous phase, take refuge in silence; there are always a few to briefly answer the teacher's more formal questions and thus allow the class to carry on, as to the others...

Ignoring a hot current event

Let us go back to an elementary class in Geneva for a last example; the teacher has chosen to study alpine passes and tunnels. A map of Switzerland with landforms, large cities, and main arteries is on the blackboard. The well-known behavior is repeated: first give the pupils a chance to talk and then find out what they already know. But it so happens that this is the Monday following the tragic fire in the Mont-Blanc Tunnel. More than 40 people have died. As far as tunnels go, the pupils' accounts do not refer to a list of "alpine gaps," but to what they saw on television. Again the tragedy, the emotions which arose from the images: burnt cars and firefighters in action. Decidedly, on this day, studying tunnels is more than a trivial school project that gravitates entirely towards a task consisting in identifying and naming passages in the Alps, placing them on a map, locating the cities and regions and their interconnections, anticipating what has to be learnt for the evaluation, for the test that will certainly focus on very declarative knowledge. Nevertheless, as in the previous example, the teacher, although momentarily destabilized by the pupils' interventions - they all have something to say - momentarily hesitant regarding the course of action to take - why not try to put these disparate remarks in order? - takes control again, not to work on this most recent direction, but to set pupils to the planned tasks. The topic is hot; its content is tragic, emotions are expressed in various ways. This does not correspond to the teacher's project. The objective pursued in letting the pupils speak was not to trigger such an avalanche of words and questions, and there are a great number of questions in every direction. Consequently, the class rapidly falls back into line, into the usual line of school exercises and practices. Emotions that were high are quieted down; they are reduced to a few individual whispers while the teacher reminds pupils of the work that needs to be done on the maps and atlases at their disposal.

In social sciences: Topics that are judged, appreciated or rejected, but never neutral

No matter the contexts and circumstances in which these stories take place, they have two features in common. On one hand, they testify to the profoundly intertwined character of knowledge with what we refer to as emotions in these disciplines, and on the other hand to the significance of this emotional dimension, by the manner in which pupils assimilate the topics they are taught. In general, several observations converge towards the importance of the manner in which pupils approach History, Geography, and Citizenship Education. There are aspects that attract and others that repel. What attracts pupils in History are, for example, aspects that can easily be identified, that refer to human characteristics and actions, that awaken strong feelings, also that are mysterious; Ancient Egypt enjoys everlasting success. However, this is not without ambiguity and we could, for example, question the admittedly troubling success of chapters on Nazism and World War II. Periods in which "nothing happens", in which formal study of institutions dominates, are rejected; Greek Democracy or the Roman Empire breed mitigated interest.

Academic knowledge is itself bearer of appreciation, which is translated into presentations where emotions are asserted. Thus, in Geography textbooks, images of Africa give great importance to the Sahel's famines or droughts and its consequences, whereas those of Latin America are comprised of a large proportion of shantytowns. The purpose is to give rise, through emotions, to questions, interrogations, and interest for the subject. Inversely, how many analyses of exercises, paintings and more broadly works of art, barely hint at aesthetic emotion or pleasure to immediately arrive at reasoned analysis, historical context and comprehension in verbal terms?

Knowledge, emotions, judgments, beliefs...

By relating these images and by introducing some questions about them, words are hesitant. Under the general term of "emotions", we have often seen or slipped in other terms that are closely or directly associated. With emotions, the subject asserts what belongs to him, to the relationships he constructs and establishes with knowledge, with the world, the present and past social world as far as we are concerned.

Rather than discussing the term "emotion" itself, we simply underline a few aspects essential to our discourse. These aspects all assert the proximity of emotions, judgments, values, and beliefs. Behind this, stands a question a thousand times dissected and studied: are human beings rational or emotional? We have too many examples, even though they are not absolute proof, to guard ourselves against such dichotomies when they are reified. We are very aware of the ideological and political choices given as reasons, which invite us to transform these choices into obligations, which are then imposed upon others. The opposite of reason is not emotion or feeling, but insanity, madness. The dictionary is sometimes misleading and the common meaning treacherous. Our judgments, more so when they refer to human actions, are never judgments of reason alone; they are mixed with emotions, attractions and repulsion, with feelings we experience towards things human, all things human. This does not mean that reason is subjected to our emotions, that all judgment is nothing but a product of the latter. Let us accept Livet's (1995) proposition, which arguments the idea that emotions form a system with beliefs, values and desires. A complex alchemy the teacher is not required to dissect or analyze, but it is important to (re)cognize so as to make room in one way or another for this dimension which is also cognitive and which, with reason, contributes to the construction of our relationship with others and the world. Let us go a little further; Gordon (1990) distinguishes emotions from feelings. For this author, emotions are shared in every culture. Fear, joy, anger, sadness, etc., are present everywhere. Feelings are corporal sensations culturally constructed and signified. The interest in such a distinction is to inform us of the fact that the expression of emotions and the meaning they are given varies according to cultures, and without doubt according to each person. It is therefore important to mistrust any reduction of a feeling expressed as a sort of generally shared meaning. As such, comprehension we have of human and social realities and phenomena is a composition of various ingredients in which emotions, judgments beliefs, values, knowledge, reason, etc. are mixed.

3. Between reject and recognition, obstacle and support

Thus, no matter the status and the place we give them, emotions are inseparable from knowledge, from subjects who construct and state knowledge, from people, pupils who receive knowledge, from teachers who teach and construct knowledge. School tradition copes with this situation as well as can be expected.

Ambiguity of school traditions

Without going back at length over ideas that prevailed when schooling was born in developed countries in the 19th century, it is important to recall the strength of reference to reason, reason which we have qualified in our introduction as the legitimacy, horizon and pedestal of teaching. Reason, said to be human beings' principal universal characteristic, is the only legitimate reference of a public school for all. It would fall into particularities without it. Reason is teaching's horizon, it contributes to forming beings of reason through mediation of exercises and academic knowledge. Reason is also teaching's pedestal in that this same academic knowledge is supposed to have been constructed and established, chosen and set in place according to processes of reason, and to stem from it. It is a question of teaching young generations not to believe just anything, to rationally examine facts, to distinguish opinion from knowledge, a notion widely developed and studied in numerous works.

Nevertheless, we cannot stop here. As it were, upstream from reason is the person, which we said could not be reduced to reason. Neither can the purposes of our disciplines be reduced to forming this being of reason. History, Geography, Citizenship Education are established in schools, first to construct collective identity. These civic functions bear a strong dose of emotions. One's country, one's homeland, ought to be loved, loved to defend it, and loved because it is supposed to bring peace and security to everyone, along with the possibility of exercising one's liberties and talents. These purposes are charged with real and assumed emotions. But all is not so simple. It is to serve reason that emotions are called upon. There are many reasons to love and defend one's country, to admire its scenery and feel proud. As to Citizenship Education, it was long referred to as Moral and Civic Instruction; the love for homeland and its political institutions is mixed with moral values that must be transmitted within the academic framework. Indoctrinated for a good cause, emotions are thus totally legitimate, all the more legitimate as the more knowledge of one's country and history increases, the more reasons to love it assert themselves...

Emotion is therefore widely present and recognized. But on the other hand, it is suspicious. It is in elementary school, with young children, that programs and other study outlines accept this dimension of emotion. Little by little, as they grow up, reason must take over completely. Emotion and what accompanies it are set aside. To do this, there are two options. The first is to question it, to interrogate it, to study the role it plays in the construction of knowledge; the second consists in rejecting it, even negating it. In secondary teaching it is principally this second option that is chosen. It is a matter of teachers explaining and pupils understanding. Explanation and comprehension, whether in History, Geography or Citizenship Education, interested solely in reasons to the detriment of emotions, to reasons that have causes, causes which are identifiable, causes with unquestionable consequences. Emotion carries a risk of prevailing over judgment, and thus the citizen becomes a person subjected to passions, incapable of reasoned choices, unable to think of the common good. Here we encounter one of the strong beliefs on which schools base themselves: more knowledge generates more judgment, a more reasoned or more reasonable action.

Short detour on the epistemology of academic knowledge

Teaching the three disciplines we refer to is therefore heavily marked by this reference to reason. Examining academic knowledge as actions, those taught in classrooms show them very "realistically"; words are things, teaching History tells the reality of the past, Geography the reality of the present on Earth's surface, Citizenship Education the reality of public life and political institutions. We are almost constantly in a sort of latent positivism. The text of knowledge is and must be stable and legal (Barthes, 1973/1995). It must be a stable text because it is meant for teaching in an institution, within a time frame, and intended for groups of pupils, beyond the singularities of schools and classrooms. It must be legal because it bears the "truth," knowledge as stated at a given moment, in regard to the topics it teaches; there are so many characteristics and reasons to hold emotions and their particularities at bay.

Furthermore, in all three disciplines, the aim is to explain. It is not a matter of knowing for knowledge's sake, but of understanding. Thus, human acts, historical events, geographical and social facts have causes. These causes are a product of reasoned, if not rational, analysis. They highlight constraints, contexts, and circumstances. Ever present in everyone's mind are the classifications that originate from distinctions between natural and human causes as regards Geography, between economic, political and cultural causes, etc. Two other factors, fate and decision are thus held at bay and with them the passions, interests, feelings, doubts and hesitations that are the very support of our social experience. History in school is overwhelmingly teleological whereas Geography in school has difficulty steering away from a tradition where a certain mostly natural determinism prevails. As to the institutions, they state principles, laws, and regulations that are applied, almost like a prescription or a poultice. This verb, "to apply" wards off any idea of interpretation and therefore the essential part of the subject that decides, judges and acts.

This situation is not a sign of deliberate choice on the part of the teachers or totally reasoned agreement to some explanatory principles. More profoundly, it translates certain characteristics of the School, such as the demands of transmitting common culture and teachers' ethical precautions. Factors that lead to warding off that which divides, causes problems, and contributes to introducing public divisions, oppositions, and opinions in the classroom. Admittedly, teachers attempt to take into account these dimensions of knowledge, of its uses and social significance, but pressure is exerted to prioritize teaching consensual knowledge.

Displacements

These notions are ever present in peoples' minds and acted out in practice. Nonetheless, certain factors suggest calling them into question and rethinking the emotional dimension in teaching and learning the three disciplines. We have assembled a few such factors around six approaches which we very briefly present.

(1) A constructivist epistemology. At present, constructivism and socio-constructivism are widespread terms used to study and orient school practice. Beyond these notions, and more broadly, there is the idea according to which we construct the world, what we know and understand of it, whether natural or social. The world is not an element that the subject deciphers in search of appropriateness between this world and its deciphering, but a construction of the subject. Words are not things; we construct the world with words and concepts at our disposal and which we use, with our languages, our ways of categorizing reality, our cultures (see Watzlawick, 1988). This constructivist position does not necessarily lead to a sort of general relativism according to which everything would be alike and equivalent. More than ever, ethical requirements are necessary and, among these the need for truth in regard to knowledge. If discourses on present and past societies are always situated from a certain point of view, and if this point of view – no matter how well reasoned and argued – always carries with it peculiarities of the subject that states and generates the discourse and therefore his values, appreciation, judgments and emotions, then it also remains to be constructed, heard and examined in regard to the value of truth. This is where scientific dialogue, but also the debate of citizens, is more than ever necessary. However, without mistaking the first for the second, and without believing or making believe that the first could supplant the second. The path is narrow.

(2) Recognizing the affective dimension in text comprehension. Comprehending a text was long thought to be a matter of deciphering the author's intentions; now it is thought to result from the activity of a subject that reads or hears the text. To comprehend means to give meaning. The reader-listener constructs this meaning according to his knowledge of the world the text refers to, the context in which he finds himself and the structure of the text. Indeed, we have what Umberto Eco calls "the rights of

the text". By this he suggests that although interpretation and comprehension of human acts always remain open, and meaning is never given and closed, all of this takes place in a defined space restrained by the text itself, the manner in which reality is constructed, and the topics covered. This activity of the subject implies affectivity and emotion. Several investigations clearly emphasize the importance of these dimensions in generating pupils' support for or refusal of such or such a chapter in History or Geography and thus make them available for study and learning.

(3) Representations and attitudes. In the last few decades, the notion according to which subjects construct their knowledge has led to consider more and more what is "already there" in the pupil's mind. Among the theoretical references most frequently used to study, construct and rest upon this "already there," Social Sciences' didactics call on Social Representations as studied and theorized by Moscovici (1976) and after him. Let us recall that one of the three dimensions of Social Representation is attitude. Attitude designates the position of the subject in relation to the topic and involves affective, judgment and emotional concerns. Several works testify to these attempts at taking into account representations in teaching. However it is interesting to note that interest for representations has spread to didactic reflection; the affective dimension is often minimized, even forgotten. Studying the information pupils have at their disposal and their method of organizing this information is widely privileged to the detriment of attitudes. When these are taken into account, they are reduced to a factor of attraction or refusal. Here again we concentrate on knowledge in its reasoned form. Fundamentally, this caution also testifies to the difficulty, on one hand, of studying this dimension of knowledge and relationships to knowledge constructed by pupils, and on the other hand, of taking it into account.

(4) Knowledge about societies within multicultural societies. Growing preoccupations linked to multiculturalism trigger another displacement in manners of considering matters of emotions. Increasing awareness of cultural diversity in our societies and the need to take this diversity into account has accentuated interest in two previously encountered complementary aspects. On the one hand, there is the culture's presence, from the perspective of world conception, social relationships, and

values inherent to any culture. On the other hand there are relationships constructed by the subject with taught topics that often differ according to conceptions and values. Everyone recognizes a common situation in which Citizenship Education opens up to studying questions of society and to debate. Conflicts in values and norms (for example, Costa-Lascoux, 1992) very rapidly appear behind divergent viewpoints and opinions. A first level of interpretation is to ascribe these conflicts, and the differences in appreciation they translate from, to cultural differences. However, the analysis must not stop there. Conflicts in culture are also social and economic conflicts. Opinions and viewpoints on the world partly depend on the knowledge people have of the topics debated, but also on experiences mobilized in regard to this knowledge. We have seen this at work in the 5th grade pupils' stories about equality. On a deeper level, we concur with the conception of law defended by an author such as Dworkin (1994) for whom any judgment, any decision, is always a choice between conflicting values.

(5) Everything not in schools that should be. Examination of various curricula shows increasing concern on all levels of teaching for topics of study regarding social preoccupations that do not easily find a place in disciplines present in school at the moment (Audigier, 2001). Transversal themes in French colleges in 1985 programs, General Education fields in Quebec programs, General and Citizenship Education fields in the study program project for French-speaking Switzerland, invitations to introduce Health, Media, and Environment Education etc., are so many orientations that translate this search for an insertion of new topics. Historically, this project is not new, but it is now asserted with much more strength, much more urgency. Beyond questions linked to the insertion of school topics into other configurations than those outlined by the usual disciplines, we note that these topics are hot, in the sense that they concern people, attitudes, and judgments. People no longer believe that reasoning about the ill effects of tobacco is enough to bring youngsters to give up the pleasure of smoking! No one believes that media education can be limited to a cold and aloof analysis of a few television programs! However, there are still difficulties when taking into account this affective, emotional subject to construct schools' horizon and reason for being, in other words a subject with a critical mind, capable of distancing himself.

(6) Approaches for a more general context. Finally, we simply suggest that these displacements exist within the scope of a more general context that must also be critically analyzed. As our societies and our ways of understanding them change so do our conceptions of social bonds; so too the Social Sciences studying them, including History, which poses today's questions of the past. Thus, for example, these sciences have been marked in the last few decades with the return of the actor. Works, already considered ancient, have doubted the fiction of a rational and perfectly informed Homo Economicus; they make room for the product of passions in the decisions the individual takes. Awarding the 2002 Nobel Prize for economics concurrently to an economist and a psychologist also expresses this evolution. The return of the actor, and calling into question this fiction of a purely rational individual, go hand in hand with the emphasis that is now placed on the person's autonomy. Proclamation of liberty as a fundamental attribute of human beings is not questioned; however, once more such an assertion should not be reified and ought to analyze both the linguistic and social contexts in which this notion of autonomy takes place. Autonomous, the subject is thus summoned to personally generate his norms and values (for example, D'Iribarne, 1996). He is responsible without restriction for his own acts and choices; totality that, in case of failure, slips from responsibility to guilt or simply to inadequacy, inadequacy in his own eyes, inadequacy in the eyes of others. All of this, other than a few familiarities with disaffiliation processes, translates refusal or ignorance of constraints, contexts, personal, and collective histories, and therefore interdependencies – through the simple fact that liberty and autonomy are not observable, are not noticeable in a person. Liberty and autonomy are a movement, a dynamic constructed throughout a lifetime. There is also much to say about effacing separations between private and public spaces, or appeals to authenticity of which we see the results in classrooms.

Should we see in these appeals for authenticity and autonomy the last manifestation of the ideal of romanticism and its notion of individual, or yet the best support for spreading an ideology that evokes social Darwinism and according to which competition between people is the best social regulator? This ideology allows a justification of the victory of the strongest and as such of all inequalities as long as the market generates them. Be that as it may, the importance now given to the subject, to the expression of his thoughts and feelings must be considered with infinite caution and a critical mind. On the one hand, nothing points to speech as personal expression, on the other hand everyone is entitled to silence, more so on what is most intimate – emotions, feelings. Neither classroom nor School ought to be constructed according to the panoptic dream. Such frequent use of the word "transparency" gives the shivers; not only is there no such thing as a transparent being since, to carry the image further, we see through him, but this dream of transparency has always been linked to totalitarian power, whether in politics, families, media or schools. There is more than paradox in claiming that the subject; the person must be placed at the forefront, and in exhibiting his feelings, emotions and desires as motivations of success in our entertainment society.

4. Working with and on emotions to acquire knowledge

Yet, driving away emotions is impossible. Relationships that pupils construct with knowledge and skills in Citizenship Education, History and Geography, not only include these individual dimensions but knowledge itself is filled with, if not constructed by these dimensions. Henceforth, this constitutes one of the starting points for a reflection on teaching and learning Social Sciences. It is not only the recognition that all discourse on present and past societies is constructed "from a certain point of view," but also that this point of view, that of the speaking, thinking, reasoning subject is comprised of an emotional dimension and is also constructed by it. Consequently, it is no longer relevant to ignore this emotional dimension, to attempt to marginalize it, or even to spare a moment for pupils to "express themselves freely" and then set it aside. Both the pupils' construction of a relationship to knowledge and critical education depend on it. If the title of the last part of this chapter separates knowledge from emotion, it is to better invite work on their conjunction, more specifically their intricacy in relation to each other.

In the construction of the relationship to knowledge that he postulates, Charlot (1997, p. 84-85) distinguishes three levels: relationship to the world; relationship to self and; relationship to others. The first refers to the relationship the subject has with the world, its topics, and the culture that is already present ... "any relationship to knowledge has an epistemic dimension." The second concerns the personal story made of desires, pleasures, interests, etc., in this relationship "construction of self and its reflexive echo, image of self, is always at work." The third underlines the "relational dimension." Just as Social Representations, such constructions invite teachers to work on different dimensions of relationships, relationships the subject has with knowledge and its construction in the classroom learning activity. Components of the relationship each person has with social topics, emotion and affective dimensions are also components of the teaching and learning situation, both with regard to form and with regard to relationships between people involved in the situation, in particular relationships between pupils and the teacher. These last two components are not dealt with here but should not be forgotten. In this chapter, we deliberately go no further than the construction of knowledge and skills in Social Sciences. We also stay solidly anchored to the purposes of intellectual and critical education, which are most essential to legitimize the presence of our disciplines in all levels of teaching. Three work orientations are presented here.

Concepts are also charged with emotions

The first work orientation focuses on construction of concepts in Social Sciences. The subject might appear a bit paradoxical since a concept is spontaneously associated with abstraction, in turn referred to reason, which is hardly "emotionalized." Nevertheless, it is by fixing this objective of concept construction that we can take emotional dimensions into account without giving up the more essential purposes of school. To do this, one must analyze with rigor and precision the concepts in question, their characteristics, and their specificity.

Our first story involved the concept of equality within the framework of a Citizenship Education assignment. Displacing its traditional methods and contents, this work focused on construction of concepts. We mentioned the almost immediate comprehension that pupils had of equality as soon as it allowed them to relate and therefore think of an actual experience. It is because of their spontaneous comprehension of equality that they were able to relate a situation of inequality they experienced, in order to judge it, here to denounce it. Inequalities are part of life. But it is because humans constructed the concept of equality and gave it, under certain circumstances, the power to become a value, a point of view, from which to evaluate and judge social realities, indeed organize them, to decide upon their actions, that certain inequalities seem acceptable. It is also because these situations are deemed unacceptable that they cause strong emotional reactions in pupils. No one can say whether reaction to a situation or spontaneous use of a concept of equality comes first. Both are probably intertwined. But the concept only takes shape in connection to singular social situations where comprehension itself involves emotion.

Here we are dealing with value-words or socio-moral concepts to take up two expressions that, each in its own way, encompasses the total interweaving of reason with emotion and judgment (see Audigier, 1991; Pagoni-Andreani, 1999). These words or concepts with which we speak about the social world have quadruple dimensions: social, legal, ethical, and political. (1) A social dimension because they are used to speak and evaluate our world, and the relationships between human beings. They are immersed in our divisions, our conflicts, our agreements, and our co-operations. (2) A legal dimension because they are linked to our laws, our rights, our obligations. These outline the framework in which we exercise our liberties. (3) An ethical dimension because they always call on moral values and norms. And finally: (4) A political dimension because, taken in the very movement of our societies, they depend upon our collective decisions. Let us stay on the concept of equality. Its social dimension is directly linked to what it allows us to say about the society in which we live. Its legal dimension is linked to the assertion of the principle of equality before the law. It is an ethical concept because it calls upon statements such as equal dignity of individuals. Finally, it is political because of its meaning, its strength and its use evolve, and they change according to decisions made within the democratic space.

We have thus come across accounts in which pupils strongly express notions of equality. Schoolwork profitably bases itself on such accounts to confront them, to share the meanings of the concept studied, to introduce other meanings with other previously specified dimensions. Case studies, human experiences, are necessary supports to study, analyze, and understand social situations, to construct concepts and tools of thought, to locate and state emotional and affective dimensions and to keep them at arm's length. This distance is not a negation of these dimensions, an error, or even an impossibility, but a means to reason about them so as to better understand them and "make do."

School experience as a support to citizenship education

The second work orientation, with the Citizenship Education example, more directly concerns relationships between knowledge and experience. Previously, we observed that one of the strong beliefs upon which our modern schools are based consists in the positive relationship between knowledge and behavior. Our intention is not to debate the wager on human beings' educability; no matter the position in this wager, we can reasonably argue that there is a greater probability that the behavior of a well-informed person will correspond. Thus, a society in which human rights are taught and known will probably be a society in which less behaviors and laws will be contrary to these rights. Furthermore, for certain values and principles to be recognized as essential for its citizens' common life and for them to refer to these values and principles for their actions, indeed for their fights, these values and principles must have been taught and constructed. The best human rights pupil can be the worst totalitarian; the one who adheres to these rights and to the values implied must know them to defend them. Although insufficient, knowledge is a necessary condition.

Although it has been said for a long time that Citizenship Education – particularly in its ethical and moral education component – should attach importance to examples, experiences, participation plans, etc., several signs indicate that a strong dichotomy too often exists between this education's teaching and pupils' experiences in schools and classrooms. More or less well documented studies and approaches now abound, some are more on the report side and underline degradation of school order by highlighting violence and incivilities, whereas others are on the remediation side and insist upon setting up speech and dialogue plans. If these plans are largely based on school experience, at the same time a topic of study and attention, in particular when there are difficulties or conflicts, and an opportunity to transform school life and foster pupils' initiatives, they seem hardly linked to construction of knowledge. It is as though experience, even though rigorously implemented, was sufficient to construct knowledge in pupils. Noting the lack of effect that formal teaching of rules, values, and principles of common life has does not entitle one to believe that experience alone is sufficient. After all, the wounded at Solferino did not know they were the emotional starting point of the Red Cross...

Here we speak in favor of school experiences as a privileged support for Citizenship Education, of the construction of concepts linked to living together, concepts that are many and rich in meanings and potentiality of actions. A few examples of concepts that can be worked and constructed in connection to school experience and the four dimensions previously mentioned include: 1) Law and matters of rules: the fact that school rule is not a product that spontaneously and freely emanates from the minds of pupils or teachers and adults. It lies within the framework of a text hierarchy and must not be contrary to principles and values that precede it are superior or exterior to it. 2) Representation: when certain pupils are designated or elected by their peers to fulfill certain functions. It includes complex questions, such as: the imperative mandate, control of constituents, protection of the representative in the exercise of his duties, etc., but also the confidence, the seduction at work when choosing a candidate, etc. 3) Reference to the law and the legal world: enabling one to work on conflict resolution, on the importance of a third party judge, of contradictory debate and text references anterior to the conflict, on sanctions and on the difference between punishment and reparation, etc. It also refers to institutions and a world of practices where we find what has already been said about value conflicts and interpretations present in any decision at work. Examples abound. They all speak in favor of the school experience – no matter what it may be – as primary work support for pupils within the framework of Citizenship Education, whose intention is also to construct knowledge. The experience thus considered can on no account be the object of nothing but a rational point of view. However keeping a distance is difficult. It requires explaining the knowledge in play, sorting out reasoned arguments and emotional or affective dimensions. It is also true that introducing these moments of distancing, of critical analysis, of knowledge formalizations is delicate. These moments are seen as difficult by a good number of pupils. First and foremost, before playing a role in fostering pupils to express themselves, teachers are carriers of knowledge and knowledge construction skills. They do not master everything, but they are supposed to help pupils find the path for this construction. They are also the ones who, particularly in public schools, convey the law, law that has been established within a democracy, and the values with which this law is not supposed to disagree. Thus, for example, prior to becoming possible topics of debate, in several democracies pedophilia and racism are crimes. Above all, the teacher's role is to recall the law.

Restore its strength to human liberty

The last orientation suggested in these few pages prolongs what has been written on the epistemology of school knowledge. Moreover, it insists on this aspect of teaching in our disciplines that is often absent, more exactly marginalized by a purely explicative will, which we refer to as human liberty, the importance of choices, of decisions. The idea of looking at everything from the viewpoint of a certain cold notion of reason very often leads to leaving this liberty aside. It is not at all a matter of submitting liberty to emotion alone, nor of setting a notion in pupils' minds that choices do not obey any rationality. Here again, the stakes in education are to distinguish, to sort, to make room for moments in which the past may have, might have swung, in which the present is not totally enclosed in necessities that would compel the future.

Many works on teaching Social Sciences, particularly in their citizenship functions, now insist on introducing the study of questions of society, on the debate and its learning. The stakes are both ethical and political. They are ethical not only because, as previously mentioned, values are always present as soon as there is talk of human experiences, but also because leaving room for emotions and reasoning them are paths toward recognizing others. For a long time, Social Science teachers have been subjected to the construction of collective identities, more specifically the identity peculiar to one's community. Today, they must learn to make room for diversity of viewpoints. In his work, *Crime and Memory*, Grosser (1986) emphasizes the importance of recognizing the suffering of others. In this regard, no nation is different from any other.

Studying questions of society is also a political stake. These questions do not have scientific solutions. In other words, the manner in which our societies will think, confront and decide upon these matters, today and tomorrow, is everyone's responsibility, not the responsibility of a handful of specialists, no matter how learned they are. Not that experts have nothing to say to citizens. But no matter what these experts' advise, citizens are the ones that must decide, must choose who they entrust with power, must orient actions to undertake. Here we find, still at work, intricacy between what seems to be mostly on the side of reason and what seems to be mostly on the side of emotions. Lesson plans and school practices are a vast landscape for the construction of work, teaching and learning plans, methods of evaluation that leave room for these questions and for what they imply in regard to Citizenship Education.

5. Conclusions

By referring to the title of an issue of *Raisons pratiques* and by mentioning Wim Wenders' film, we have clearly stated that, without emotions, our world would be gray, indeed of a tone of gray that hardly stands out. Without emotion, rational thinking, or reason, however constructed, also remains in this colorlessness. Emotions and the feelings, affectivity, values, and the judgments they carry with them are life itself. But this does not qualify them to be sweet companions of teaching. With emotions we also have human passions, claims of recognition, people's involvement, pleasure but also suffering, desire but also refusal, what we sometimes believe is shared and so often divides and opposes us. We have thus underlined how difficult and delicate it is to take them into account in teaching.

Nevertheless, even if a visit into the history of our schools reveals that reason was long thought to control this dimension, the solutions of the time, and the orientations suggested, no longer suffice. It is important to take emotions into account, to make room for them, as a condition for the construction of meaning. But recognizing emotions is neither inviting their systematic expression, nor granting them privileged status. It is the knowledge, understanding, and skills taught, the relationships pupils construct with this knowledge that must be reasoned, including the emotions involved. Learning to distinguish them and differentiate what seems linked, learning to distance oneself so as to equally understand knowledge itself and the relationships one constructs with the social world is important. Reflexive and critical distancing is part of the construction of the individual.

In this chapter, we have dealt with three disciplines grouped under the general term of "Social Sciences". They bring together a wide span of use in society. If History appears mostly linked to the formation of our collective imaginations, of our notions of life in common, of the past, the present and the future of communities to which we belong, then at the other extremity, Citizenship Education is presented as principally gravitating towards the construction of social skills, of behaviors in society. Between the two, Geography is a construction of both world representations and practical tools that are supposed to help master certain acts, such as displacements. Beyond these differences, the three are joined in the intimacy, in the interweaving of epistemic, social and affective dimensions of the knowledge they generate, in the manner in which subjects receive, hear, understand and learn this knowledge. It is because at each extremity of the long hike between scientific and academic constructions and their construction by pupils, these different dimensions are present and interrelated that they must be given prominence. It is because the school project in a democracy is the construction of a free and responsible person that critical education is at the heart of these three disciplines' teaching. Emotions are components of knowledge; the work and reflection necessary to identify and understand the role they play in knowledge, in our conceptions, in our imaginaries, so as not to be subjected to them, is a vast landscape to open and achieve.

References

Audigier, F., & G. Lagelée (1996). *L'initiation juridique dans l'éducation civique des colleges.* Paris: INRP.

Audigier, F. (1991). Enseigner la société, transmettre des valeurs; former des citoyens, éduquer aux droits de l'homme: une mission ancienne, des problèmes permanents, un projet toujours actuel, *Revue Française de Pédagogie, 94,* 37-48.

Audigier, F. (2001). Les contenus d'enseignement plus que jamais en question. In I.C.G.e.S.L. (Eds.), *La formation fondamentale, un espace à redéfinir* (pp. 141-192). Montreal: Les Editions Logiques.

Barthes, R. (1973/1995). Texte (théorie du), *Encyclopedia Universalis, 22,* 370-374.

Charlot, B. (1997). *Du rapport au savoir.* Paris: Anthropos.

Costa-Lascoux, J. (1992). L'enfant, citoyen à l'école, *Revue française de pédagogie, 101,* 71-78.

D'Iribarne, P. (1996). *Vous serez tous des maîtres*. Paris: Seuil.
Dworkin, R. (1994). *L'empire du droit*. Paris: Presses Universitaires de France.
Gordon, R.M. (1990). *The Structure of Emotions: Investigations in Cognitive Philosophy*. Cambridge: Cambridge University Press.
Grosser, A. (1986). *Le crime et la mémoire*. Paris: Flammarion.
Lautier, N. (1997). *À la rencontre de l'histoire*. Lille: Presses Universitaires Septentrion.
Lautier, N. (2001). Les enjeux de l'apprentissage de l'histoire, *Perspectives documentaires en éducation, 53*, 61-68.
Livet, P. (1995). Évaluation et apprentissage des emotions. In P. Paperman & R. Ogien (Eds.), *Raisons pratiques, La couleur des pensées, Vol. 6* (pp. 119-144). Paris: Éditions de l'École des Hautes Études en Sciences Sociales.
Martins, D. (1993). *Les facteurs affectifs dans la compréhension et la mémorisation des texts*. Paris: Presses Universitaires de France.
Moscovici, S. (1976). *La psychanalyse, son image, son public*. Paris: Presses Universitaires de France. (1st edition, 1961).
Pagoni-Andreani, M. (1999). *Le développement socio-moral: des théories à l'éducation civique*. Lille: Presses Universitaires Septentrion.
Ricoeur, P. (1983-1985). *Temps et récit*. Paris: Seuil.
Robert, F. (1999). *Enseigner le droit à l'école*. Paris: ESF.
Tutiaux-Guillon, N. (1998). Dans la classe: l'influence du modèle pédagogique sur l'explicatif. In F. Audigier (Ed.), *Contributions à l'étude de la causalité et des productions des élèves dans l'enseignement de l'histoire et de la géographie*. Paris: INRP.
Watzlawick, P. (1988). *L'invention de la réalité*. Paris: Seuil.

---

[1] Given the author's previous experience and his current work, examples originate from France and Geneva. Grading differs according to school systems. Both French examples were taken in the 5th grade of lower secondary college with pupils aged 12-13 years, and in the 3rd grade, with pupils aged 14-15 years. Both examples from Geneva were taken in the 6th grade of elementary school with pupils aged 11-12 years, and in the 5th grade with pupils aged 10-11 years.

[2] On the importance of intrigue in history see Ricœur (1983-1985), particularly chapter 1; in teaching, see Lautier (1997; 2001) for example.

[3] For an introduction to the two important juridical traditions, positivism and interpretation, incarnated by Kelsen and Dworkin, see Robert (1999).

[4] On the role of affective factors, Martins (1993), in history Tutiaux-Guillon (1998).

CHAPTER 5

Enhancing enjoyment in learning at school

Michaela Gläser-Zikuda and Philipp Mayring

1. Introduction

A team of researchers and teachers at the University of Education Ludwigsburg, Germany, analyzes a videotape of a school lesson in an 8th grade classroom. The topic of the German language class is grammar (punctuation). The teacher wants the students to learn punctuation by writing a letter of application. He starts the lesson:

T: "Okay, you know that you have to apply for a job soon. Many of you already started to do so, for some of you it won't be easy. It is very important to get done a correct letter of application."
S: (murmuring, talking confusedly)
T: "Here I have an example of a letter of application (transparency). Looks okay at first sight. Do you notice something?"
S: (reading the text, silent)
T: "I would say the author of this text certainly doesn't get any job."

The team is looking at this video section and reflects on students' thoughts and feelings in this situation.

S1: "Hey, this makes fun. I want to answer the riddle. Who finds out the mistakes?" (Enjoyment).
S2: "Oh no, I think I have no chance to get a job. I'm bad in writing orthographically correct." (Despair).

S3: "Oh, this is difficult. I don't have any idea what is wrong in this text. I have to pay attention to get an apprenticeship."(Anxiety).

S4: "Ah, I already know it. There are comma missing. I think I'm the first who noticed that!"(Pride).

S5: "Let's see whether I will find it out what is wrong here. Finally I have to write such a letter, too. And it is important to me to get a job."(Interest).

S6: "Oh no, I have already found a job. So what! It's lulling!" (Boredom).

Other feelings may be experienced in this situation as well. It is obvious that instruction may cause various emotions of students. We presume that learning processes are conclusively influenced by emotions.

2. Emotions

As we have seen emotions strongly vary depending on person and situation. This chapter will try to clarify what emotions are and how they relate to motivation which is a central concept in research on learning and achievement.

What are emotions?

Theoretically there is still no homogeneous definition of emotions. Generally one may say that *emotion is a general term for subjective emotional states, moods and emotional attitudes, or the state of a person experiencing a change affecting the subject's needs, goals or concerns* (cf. Ulich & Mayring, 1992; Otto, Euler & Mandl, 2000; Pekrun, 1994). Emotions occur in different areas:

- Subjective and affective experience, positive and negative arousal,
- Cognitive appraisal, evaluation of the situation and of personal affection,
- Physiological changes (neuronal, hormonal),
- Expression of behavior (miming, gesticulating) and action tendency (e.g. fight or flight).

Different theories try to explain the meaning of emotions in relation to human life. *A psychoevolutionary theory* postulates that emotions play an important role for survival (e.g. turning away when disgusted; flight when anxious). Human behavior is restricted to adaptive, biological functions within these concepts. *Cognitive emotion theories* assume that emotions are consequences of cognitive appraisals (e.g. blame as consequence of the evaluation of one's own behavior in sense of breaking accepted rules; aggression as consequence when personal impulses were impeded). Spontaneous and irrational emotional tendencies are hard to explain using these theories. *Psychoanalytical concepts* describe emotions as expression of unconscious desires (enjoyment and rage as expression of sexual and aggressive desires). These concepts confine a variety of emotions. *Phenomenological theories* reject the mentioned concepts as one-sided functional and emphasize that emotions are an enlargement of human abilities of experience. Indeed they may not explain the relationship between emotions and behavior.

So, we see that in respect to a definition of emotion, numerous theoretical concepts coexist. Therefore, today *integrative concepts* for the explanation of emotions are preferred which combine the different aspects of emotional experience (cf. Scherer, 1988).

The relationship between emotion and motivation

In educational psychology motivation theories revealed the important role of emotions (Weiner, 1986). In the middle of the last century, empirical studies already showed that hope of success and little fear of failure are a decisive impulse of achievement motivation. Further analyses showed that enjoyment and, above all, pride are motivating factors in connection with success. In contrast, feelings of shame and blame are de-motivating and suggest failure.

A modern concept of motivation is the *FLOW-Theory* (Csikszentmihalyi, 1997). Several studies suggest that persons who show maximum performance, as for example mountain-climbers, surgeons or chess-players, get into a joyful and flowing emotional state during performance. People who are intrinsically motivated and deeply absorbed in their action report on forgetting time and place. Individual abilities and demands of task are in optimal balance if neither anxiety (demands are too high) nor boredom (demands are too low) are experienced.

Another recent concept of motivation is the *Theory of Self-Determination* (Deci & Ryan, 1994). The authors postulate that social integration, experience of competence and autonomy are basic human needs.

Interest Theory, which is understood as a motivation concept, emphasizes the importance of emotions (Renninger et al., 1992). Being interested in a topic or subject means not only being curious (cognitive component), and attaching importance to it (evaluative component), but also having pleasure in the object of interest (emotional component).

As explained in all these theoretical concepts of motivation, emotions are a strong component. Positive feelings for a topic or subject matter enhance motivation, ability to deal with it and finally facilitate successful learning. As many teachers certainly know, it is difficult to teach students who are less or not motivated to learn. Thus learning without emotions is condemned to be unsuccessful.

3. Emotions, learning and achievement

Research on learning and teaching revealed that emotions play an important role in learning and achievement situations. Emotions in the context of learning and achievement can be differentiated in respect to task or social components of learning (Pekrun, 1992a, 1992b). In the following, a theoretical model and results from different empirical studies are described to illustrate the relation of emotions, learning and achievement.

Emotions in learning and achievement situations

Talking about emotions in the context of learning and achievement, one has to differentiate between emotions which are, on the one hand, related to task, and on the other, to social aspects. Pekrun (1998) describes the following emotions shown in table 1.

Table 1
Classification of learning and achievement emotions (Pekrun, 1998)

Task-related	Positive emotions	Negative emotions
Process-oriented	Enjoyment when learning	Boredom
Prospective	Hope Anticipation	Anxiety Despair
Retrospective	Enjoyment about results Relief Pride	Sadness Disappointment Shame / Guilt
Social	Gratitude Empathy Admiration Sympathy	Anger Envy Disdain Antipathy / Hate

Table 2
Frequency of students' emotions with respect to learning and achievement situations expressed as percentage (Pekrun, 1998).

Emotion	Instruction	Learning	Exam	Feedback
Enjoyment	18.4	15.6	10.0	16.0
Hope	1.6	1.2	4.8	5.6
Interest	4.9	2.7	2.8	2.2
Satisfaction	0.8	3.9	1.4	3.0
Relief	16.3	15.6	15.5	9.0
Pride	0.4	5.9	3.5	5.2
Anger	6.5	5.9	9.0	15.3
Anxiety	9.4	5.5	30.0	16.0
Hopelessness	0.0	0.8	0.7	2.2
Disappointment	2.0	1.2	2.4	10.8
Dissatisfaction	5.3	19.5	1.4	0.3
Boredom	13.5	2.7	0.3	0.0
Shame	1.2	2.3	0.0	1.1
Negative Emotions	44.5	46.4	49.3	47.0
Positive Emotions	46.5	51.2	44.1	44.8

Within task-related emotions, the differentiation between prospective, retrospective and process-oriented emotions is important in respect to specific aspects of learning and instruction. The main focus of this section is to describe and explain instructional and methodological possibilities enhancing emotions in the classroom, especially enjoyment in learning.

But which emotions are experienced in learning and achievement situations? Pekrun (1998) asked students how they feel in specific situations, for example during instruction and before and after test situations. Table 2 shows a large variety of different positive and negative emotions reported by students in learning and achievement situations.

Looking closely at the results, one can see that not only is anxiety being experienced often, but also that positive emotions such as hope, relief and enjoyment are reported at a comparable rate. For a long time, most of the research in the field of learning and achievement has focused on anxiety (Zeidner, 1998). It is well analyzed that anxiety has a negative impact on learning. In recent years, several empirical studies have started to investigate more on positive emotions.

Experimental studies, for example, analyze the influence of mood on information processing and problem solving. Emotions are seen as a kind of switching position for attention and thinking processes (Fiedler, 1988; Isen, 1987). In respect to thinking, a sequential-analytical style of thinking is differentiated from an intuitive-holistic style. Negative mood is linked with a more concentrated, logically oriented, detailed and controlled process of thinking. While positive mood promotes creative, flexible and fluent thinking, improvement of memorizing, and acceleration of problem solving. These results are important for the discussion of instructional methods as will be explained later.

The importance of enjoyment in learning

Certainly there is no educator or teacher who is not convinced of the fact that joyful learning is an essential precondition for successful learning. It is astonishing that real instruction often lacks enjoyment. Depending on personal school experience and public opinion that learning is hard work and has nothing to do with enjoyment, instruction and learning are connected with feelings of displeasure for many people. Teachers, in fact, know that many students are only happy when there is no school.

Not only in every day school life is enjoyment missing when talking about learning, but as well in educational science. Very rarely will one find the term enjoyment in an encyclopedia or compendia of educational science. Enjoyment is a fundamental criterion in education. The central task of education and instruction, with assistance from an educator or teacher, is to facilitate students become competent in dealing with of criticism and judgment in a mature way. A student is only prompted for learning, unfolds towards a topic, when interested in and joyful about the topic. Beyond that, it is important for the learner to have success and to know that it makes sense to learn. Enjoyment is a strong and important driving force in human life. This does not mean that enjoyment at school and in learning should be evoked by using jokes or educational tricks. But education and learning at school should be characterized by a humanistic basis which focuses on attentiveness, appreciation, encouragement and consolation.

With respect to empirical outcomes, the studies on learning emotions of Pekrun (1998), mentioned before, illustrate that besides hope and relief, enjoyment is the main emotion experienced in learning situations in the classroom. In our studies (Gläser-Zikuda, 2001; Laukenmann et al., 2003), we found enjoyment strongly related to achievement and motivation. A sample of 650 students of secondary school level (8th grade) was questioned about emotions (anxiety, anger, boredom, well-being, enjoyment, satisfaction and interest), motivation, classroom climate and cognitive aspects of learning (self-concept, learning strategies, pre-knowledge, test results) in two subjects' areas (language and science / physics). Additionally, a small part of these students (N = 24) were interviewed and reported on feelings and teaching/learning styles in a diary log for a period of 6 weeks.

The analysis of diaries and interviews shows that positive emotions, enjoyment and interest, refer mainly to experiences of competence and success in connection with learning. Based on results from the questionnaires positive correlations between achievement and well-being (differentiated as enjoyment and satisfaction) as well as interest are highly significant. The outcome of this is that attention should be paid to the role of emotions for learning and achievement.

4. Emotions in classroom and instruction

Looking at classroom interaction emotions play an important role. Perception and regulation of personal emotions as well as perception and adequate reaction about emotions from others is generally a crucial aspect in human communication, and most importantly, classroom interactions.

Another point which should be considered with respect to learning and teaching is how emotions relate to instruction. Are there possibilities that can be focused on that will enhance emotions in the classroom?

Regulation of emotions - the importance of emotional intelligence

A theory which focuses on emotional processes is "Emotional Intelligence" (Salovey & Mayer, 1990). In his popular book with the same cover Daniel Goleman made use of this theoretical approach (Goleman, 1995). Emotional Intelligence, abbreviated EQ, refers to the intelligent dealing with the feelings of self and others. This refers to the existing understanding of intelligence which above all stresses the cognitive aspects of being able to perform while ignoring social and emotional stimuli. With respect to the theory of Emotional Intelligence, the main question is whether people make use of their emotions and moods to adapt their behavior effectively to specific circumstances of a situation. For some people, emotions are a strong load, while others are able to deal with their feelings easily and in an intuitive way.

Theoretically, different components of Emotional Intelligence can be distinguished. Emotional Intelligence includes three aspects: 1) interpretation and expression, 2) regulation and 3) productive use of emotions. The first aspect refers to an important fact in human communication. The ability to know and express one's own feelings and to interpret emotions of other people correctly facilitates fundamental verbal and non-verbal communication. In psychological therapy, this ability is also known as empathy (Rogers, 1992). The second aspect of Emotional Intelligence is to employ strategies of emotional regulation, for example, to search for another place during an emotionally difficult situation or being able to communicate in a sad or depressing situation. The third aspect mentioned above is the most relevant in respect to learning and instruction.

Because emotions are related to cognitive processes, emotional intelligent persons use their knowledge about the influence of emotions to influence thinking style, memory, creativity, motivation and readiness to risk. Their planning is flexible and includes various possibilities in problem solving. For example, some teachers prefer coming home from school and completing housework instead of immediately planning lessons. Clearly structured and automated work leads to feelings of satisfaction and improves personal mood. Afterwards planning for school which requires creative thinking may be easier. It is the same for the student who does not make any progress in preparation for a test. Playing outside or reading a good book for a while influences mood positively. Thinking processes, which are needed to understand, compile and to memorize topics, accelerate increasing productivity.

Mayer and Salovey (1997) argue that capabilities for emotional intelligent behavior are acquirable. This is in fact a central point for education. Table 3 shows some specific strategies in educational context to enhance Emotional Intelligence. The four branches of the diagram are arranged from the most basic psychological processes to higher and more integrated processes. For example, the lowest level branch describes the simple abilities of perceiving and expressing emotion. In contrast, the highest level branch describes the conscious, reflective regulation of emotion.

Each branch described using four abilities. Abilities that emerge early in development are to the left of the branch. Later developing abilities are to the right. Later abilities emerge within a more integrated adult personality and are consequently less distinct. These abilities apply to internal, personal emotions and the emotions of others. People, who are of high emotional intelligence, are expected to progress more quickly through, and to master, the abilities described above

For teaching Emotional Intelligence, for example, Akin et al. (1993) developed specific material. One may find helpful ideas and exercises to plan lessons on topics like "expression of personal emotions" or "getting to know my feelings of anxiety" in this teacher handbook.

Table 3
Skills in emotional intelligence (Mayer & Salovey, 1997)

Reflective regulation of emotions to promote emotional and intellectual growth			
Ability to stay open to feelings, both those that are pleasant and those that are	Ability to reflectively engage or detach from an emotion depending upon its judged informative ness or utility.	Ability to reflectively monitor emotions in relation to oneself and others, such as recognizing how clear, typical, influential, or reasonable	Ability to manage emotion in oneself and others by moderating negative emo-tions and en-hancing pleasant ones, with-out repressing or exaggerating information they may convey.

Understanding and analyzing emotions: Employing emotional knowledge			
Ability to label emotions and recognize the relationship among the words and the emotions themselves, such as the relationship between liking and loving.	Ability to interpret the meanings that emotions convey regarding relationships, such as that sadness often accompanies a loss.	Ability to understand complex feel-ings: simultaneous feelings of love and hate, or blends such as awe as a combination of fear and sur-prise.	Ability to recognize likely transitions among emotions, such as the transition from anger to satisfaction, or from anger to shame.

Emotional facilitation of thinking			
Emotions prioritize thinking by directing attention to important information.	Emotions are sufficiently vivid and utilized as aids for judgment and memory using feelings.	Emotional mood swings change the individual's per-spective from optimistic to pessimistic, encouraging consideration of multiple points of view.	Emotional states differentially encourage specific problem approaches such as when happiness facilitates inductive reasoning and creativity.

Perception, appraisal, and expression of emotion			
Ability to identify emotion in one's physical states, feelings, and thoughts.	Ability to identify emotions in other people, designs, artwork, etc., through language, sound, appearance, and behavior.	Ability to express emotions accurately and to express needs related to those feelings.	Ability to discriminate between accu-rate and inac-curate, or honest versus dishonest ex-pression of feeling.

Emotional oriented methods of instruction

Besides perception and regulation of emotions and mood on the level of social relationship there are several possibilities for designing instruction more emotional oriented (Astleitner, 2000). First of all we should focus on connection of learning topics to emotional experiences. Topics which have a meaning to students are emotional related to students' learning objectives, concepts and prior knowledge. Knowledge which has an emotional relevance for the learner probably will be memorized and transferred on problem solving easier than isolated facts like for example historical years or mathematical formula.

The phenomena described above are known as 'sluggish knowledge'. To counter this kind of knowledge the concept of 'situated learning' was developed. In the beginning of the last century, aspects of this concept were claimed in education. Learning, in respect to current and self determined problems, is strongly connected to personal concepts and objectives. Relationships to everyday life are important and should be taken into account by the teacher. These may be hobbies, family experience or topics discussed in peer group (music, friendship etc.). Students should have the chance to look for interesting topics, to formulate questions in respect to the topic and to work at a self-regulated pace while solving tasks.

Another important aspect is to learn with as many senses as possible. This would include not only to hear about a topic, but to see, smell, and manipulate it as well. In that way, emotional experiences are made enabling a connection between the knowledge and the emotional impression. Furthermore, when dealing with learning, students may remember similar experiences or what was already learned when the memory is evoked.

A link between emotions and topics facilitates learning. The mood of the learner, his way of thinking and demands of a task should fit together. The way we think while learning strongly depends on our mood in a certain situation. When in a good mood, we think in an intuitive – holistical way. A good mood signals that a situation is in order and thoughts may run without exact control. This creates advantages especially for creating ideas and for intuitive thinking. With respect to learning strategies, these situations postulate more superficial ways of learning and information processes.

On the other hand, when we are in bad mood we think more sequential – analytically. Processes of thinking are very controlled and follow a step by step procedure. In this situation, tasks are more appropriate when they allow for a systematic and routine process of procedure. When planning lessons, a teacher should pay attention to an optimal balance between students' mood and the quality of tasks. In teacher dominated instructional phases, the dominating mood in classroom is relevant for the run of lesson. But results of research on mood suggest student oriented instruction. To balance personal mood and way of thinking, students should have the opportunity to choose the task and the procedure for completing the task. By utilizing these competencies which correspond to the individual cognitive and emotional preconditions learning processes are enhanced.

Within an optimal balance between task and individual competencies students may experience "flow" (Csikszentmihalyi, 1997). A clear structure of demands, tasks and objectives promote this experience of forgetting time and place, increases positive emotions and delays wrapping up when dealing with the topic. This includes the learner often getting quick feedback during learning progress. This may be reached by media which allow self-control. Goleman (1995) describes these conditions for flow-experience as neither boring nor frightening.

In this context, motivational aspects shouldn't be negotiated. Motivation is less important in the first phase of instruction when new topics are presented. By contrast it is more important during the whole learning process. Students are more successful during learning when they are interested in a topic and emotions are positively engaged. This may be reached by instructional methods which allow self-regulated and self-determined learning. Instructional methods focusing on students' activity are different from student-centered or open structured concepts. Some of these concepts, for example weekly working plans, learning centers, play-oriented methods and project-oriented work, will be described in the following section.

Historically student-centered conceptions are anchored within reform oriented educational approaches beginning towards the end of 19th century to the beginning of the 20th century (Montessori, Freinet, Petersen, Kerschensteiner; see Morsy, 1997). Central aspects are the focus on the child with its cognitive, emotional and social needs, such as: self-activity, cooperation and creativity. The concept of weekly working plans focuses on individualized learning processes. In the working plan, a week's worth of work is described for different subjects. A part of the plan should include compulsory and voluntary tasks. Students have the opportunity to chose between different tasks on a topic, and then decide which sequence they work on tasks and how to control themselves. Working procedure, duration of work and breaks are planned individually by students. This allows students to pay attention to personal emotions and moods. Teachers are partners, supervisors, and advisors to the learning processes.

In a similar way, students decide on the order and duration of work when working with learning centers. One topic is presented in total at some centers which are placed in the classroom for the whole lesson or even a teaching unit. Different kinds of tasks are offered, for example getting information from a text, doing experiments, drawing diagrams or discussing certain aspects with a partner. Traditional working media such as worksheets, books and exercise books are used as well as experimental material, and new media (Personal Computer). This method may be appropriate to introduce a new topic using a more discovery oriented method or even for exercise reasons to consolidate knowledge and skills. By using this method, it is not only possible to focus on one subject, but several. For example, in a science learning center, a topic like cereals may have parts which focus on biological, chemical, geographical, physical and also language aspects.

Project-oriented instruction is considered to be the most demanding open structured method. Students are involved in every phase of the process. First they decide, together with the teacher, the topic of the project and the organization working process. Tasks for all participants are discussed and distributed. During the process of the project, students work at a self-guided and self-regulated pace in which the teacher takes the role of an adviser. The final step in a project is often a specific product which fulfills a useful function in everyday life. Using the project oriented learning approach, the students broaden their competencies and knowledge, enjoy the experience, and have satisfaction and pride about their performance and the results. What they learned is connected with positive emotions, making the topic easily remembered and transferred.

Finally, play oriented ways of learning are another instructional possibility to enhance positive emotions. Different kinds of play, such as role playing or quizzing, help students be active and emotional engaged in learning topics. Basically, play is a way of activity which is connected with emotional experiences, imaginative processes and phenomena described within flow theory: correspondence of task demands and personal abilities as well as forgetting time and place. While playing a learning quiz in classroom, students may experience these aspects.

With respect to role playing, emotions are experienced as well. Students deal with the topic and are enabled to take the perspective of others, including understanding their emotional behavior and regulating their own emotions. This is described in the theory of emotional intelligence (Salovey & Mayer, 1990). Having its roots in humanistic psychology, role playing is a concept which aims at self-determined and responsive behavior when dealing with the role behavior. Dealing with different ways of thinking, views and interpretations of emotions are experienced and shared with others. This concept demands expression, interpretation and regulation of emotions and contributes to enhancement of emotional intelligence.

Emotional learning

Emotions and mood are not only relevant with respect to personal relations and methodological considerations; they may be the main objective of instruction. An approach closely related to the theory of "Emotional Intelligence" is the "Self-Science Curriculum", which is implemented in numerous American schools (Stone & Dillehunt, 1978; Stone McCown et al., 1998). For nearly twenty years, the "Self-Science Curriculum" is in practice and is considered to be an appropriate model for teaching emotional intelligence. The Director of the Nueva Learning Center, Karen Stone McCown, explains:

"When we deal with rage, children learn to understand, that almost every time it is a secondary reaction, and that they have to prove what there is at the bottom of it. Are you feeling hurt? Are you jealous? Our students learn that you always have several possibilities to react on an emotion, and that life is the richer the more possibilities you know to react on an emotion" (Stone McCown in Goleman, 1995, p. 336).

The catalogue of topics dealt with in Self-Science corresponds with the components of the theory of Emotional Intelligence. Central topics of the Self-Science Curriculum are self perception (observing oneself and recognizing personal feelings), dealing with emotions (recognizing what caused the emotion and regulation), empathy (understanding emotions of others and putting oneself in the position of others), communication (development of a vocabulary of emotions and talking with others about feelings), group dynamics (knowing why and when changing positions in a group) and solving conflicts (discussing fairly problems with others).

Students don't get any grades in Self-Science; the final exam is the life in person. At the end of 8th grade, each student has to complete a "Sokrates-Exam", an oral exam in Self-Science. One task was, for example, to tell some possibilities to get along with stress, wrath, and fear. Another task is to describe an appropriate reaction helping a friend to solve a problem he has with others who push him to take drugs.

A lesson in Self-Science may deal with recognition of emotions. It is a decisive ability being able to denominate emotions and by that to differentiate better between them. While preparing the lesson students had to collect pictures of faces that show emotions. The students then had to describe and identify emotions they recognized. In the lesson, the teacher writes the emotions the students identified on the blackboard. When asked how they felt when they experienced these emotions, like anger, the students answered very quickly with "Confused", "You are not able to think clearly" and "Just bad". Afterwards, the students get a worksheet where basic emotional expressions are shown on different faces of boys and girls. Happiness, sadness, anger, surprise, anxiety and revulsion are described in respect to activity of facial muscles. For example, being anxious may have a picture of a boy with his mouth open, eyes wide open and the brow drawn up, with the eyebrows contracted, and the forehead frowning in the middle. Students imitate these emotional expressions and discuss their signal effect on people. That instruction, which deals with emotions, may be effective against a lack of emotional development. Some students, who often beat others on the school ground, may be interpreting neutral facial messages as hostile. Other students, mainly girls, may show an eating disorder because they are not able to distinguish between anger, anxiety or even hunger.

5. Conclusions

As described in this chapter, research in educational psychology revealed that learning is influenced by cognitive and emotional factors. Looking at learning at school, empirical studies have shown that a variety of negative and positive emotions are reported by students. Numerous approaches emphasize the importance of emotions in learning, for example, the flow-theory and the concept of emotional intelligence. Emotions have an influence on motivation, creativity, flexibility, and integrated thinking processes. They are highly correlated with interest, task related effort, and also, what seems to be most important, with daily instruction, and study achievement. Therefore, how emotions can be influenced during instruction is an important question for teachers and educators.

Generally speaking, it should be considered how any instruction might be designed more emotionally oriented. When planning and organizing instruction, teachers should take into account that topics, students' prior knowledge and learning activities are strongly linked to students' emotions. Demands of task, students' abilities, mood and thinking style should be matched in instructional arrangements. Different methodological approaches aim at teaching students to be self-regulated during the learning process. Within specific learning arrangements, like project oriented learning, individuals have the possibility to organize their learning steps in respect to personal abilities and mood.

Another way of enhancing students' emotions is to influence them directly. As in the theory of "Emotional Intelligence", emotions may also be a goal of instruction. Numerous schools in the United States already practice successfully instruction called "Self-Science".

Emotions of students, as well those of teachers, are important for learning and teaching at school. Future considerations in educational science and teaching methodology should take emotions into account to foster and improve successful students' learning processes.

References

Akin, T., Cowan, D., Palomares, S., & Schuster, S. (1993). *Feelings are Facts. Helping Kids understand, manage, and learn from their feelings*. Torrance, CA: Innerchoice Publishing.

Astleitner, H. (2000). Designing emotionally sound instruction: The FEASP-approach. *Instructional Science, 28*, 169-198.

Csikszentmihalyi, M. (1997). *Finding flow: the psychology of engagement with everyday life*. New York: Basic Books.

Deci, E. L., & Ryan, R. M. (1994). Promoting Self-Determined Education. *Scandinavian Journal of Educational Research, 38*(1), 3-14.

Fiedler, (1988). Emotional mood, cognitive style, and behavior regulation. In K. Fiedler, & J. Forgas (Eds.), *Affect, cognition, and social behavior* (pp. 100-119). Göttingen: Hogrefe.

Gläser-Zikuda, M. (2001). Emotions and Learning Strategies at School – Opportunities of Qualitative Content Analysis. In M. Kiegelmann (Ed.), *Qualitative Research in Psychology* (pp. 32-50). Schwangau: Huber.

Goleman, D. (1995). *Emotional Intelligence. Why it can matter more than IQ?* New York: Bantam.

Isen, A. M. (1987). Positive affect, cognitive processes, and social behavior. In L. Berkowitz (Ed.), *Advances in experimental social psychology*, Vol. 20 (pp. 203 - 253). San Diego: Academic Press.

Laukenmann, M., Bleicher, M., Fuß, S., Gläser-Zikuda, M., Mayring, Ph., & v. Rhöneck, Chr. (2003). An investigation on the influence of emotions on learning in physics. *International Journal of Science Education, 25*(4), 489-507.

Morsy, Z. (Ed.) (1997). *Thinkers on Education*, Vol. 2. Paris: UNESCO.

Otto, J. H., Euler, H.A., & Mandl, H. (2000). *Emotionspsychologie*. Weinheim: Beltz.

Pekrun, R. (1992a). Kognition und Emotion in studienbezogenen Lern- und Leistungssituationen: Explorative Analysen. *Unterrichtswissenschaft, 4*, 308-324.

Pekrun, R. (1992b). The impact of emotions on learning and achievement: Towards a theory of cognitive / motivational mediators. *Applied Psychology, 41*(4), 359-376.

Pekrun, R. (1994). Emotional development. In T. Husen, & T. N Postlethwaite, (Eds.) *The international encyclopedia of education*. Vol. 5 (pp. 1963-1967). Oxford: Elsevier (2nd edition)

Pekrun, R. (1998). Schüleremotionen und ihre Förderung. Ein blinder Fleck der Unterrichtsforschung. *Psychologie in Erziehung und Unterricht, 44,* 230-248.

Renninger, K. A., Hidi, S., & Krapp, A. (Eds.) (1992). *The role of interest in learning and development.* Hillsdale, NJ: Erlbaum.

Rogers, C. R. (1992). The necessary and sufficient conditions of therapeutic personality change. *Journal of Consulting and Clinical Psychology,* 60(6), 827-32.

Salovey, P., & Mayer, J.D. (1990). *Emotional Intelligence. Imagination, Cognition and Personality,* 9(3), 185-211.

Scherer, K. (Ed.) (1988). *Faces of emotion. Recent research.* Hillsdale: Erlbaum.

Stone K. F., & Dillehunt, H. Q. (1978). *Self-Science: The subject is me.* Santa Monica: Goodyear.

Stone McCown, K., Jensen, A. L., Freedman, J. M., & Rideout, M. C. (1998). *Self-Science. The emotional intelligence curriculum.* San Mateo, CA: Six Seconds.

Ulich, D., & Mayring, Ph. (1992). *Psychologie der Emotionen.* Grundriss der Psychologie, Band 5. Stuttgart: Kohlhammer.

Weiner, B. (1986). *An attributional theory of motivation and emotion.* New York: Springer.

Zeidner, M. (1998). Test anxiety. *The state of the art.* New York: Plenum.

CHAPTER 6

Opening doors through enhanced decision-making skills: Preparing young adolescents for healthy futures

Jeanneine P. Jones and Dawson R. Hancock

1. Introduction

From relationships to homework to double-jumping rope, early adolescents are perfect examples of the term "developmental diversity." George (1991, p.4) reminds us that they "...have little in common but the fact of changing development itself," and every educator can testify to that truth. For instance, it's not at all unusual to walk into an eighth grade classroom of fourteen-year-olds and find boys who are over six feet tall and those who have to stretch to hit five. It's just as likely that you'll spot girls who are in the final stages of physical development and those who still resemble fourth graders. You'll also see students who find complicated mathematical equations a challenging puzzle and those who struggle with the most concrete of applications. The following examples may be considered as an illustration of this developmental diversity:

> The two girls huddled over by the corner of the building, oblivious to the whoops and yells of the pre-school conversations that surrounded them. They were completely absorbed in last night's scenario:
>
> "What'd she mean by that? I can't BELIEVE she had the nerve to say that to you! Who does she think she is? Of COURSE he likes you better than her! It's not your fault she couldn't keep him interested. What'd she expect? Of all the... Hey look, there's Tonya and Rhonda. Let's tell them. They'll say I'm right. Oh wait, Mr. Brown's taking them inside. Hey Tonya, meet us in the bathroom at break. You won't BELIEVE what that little jerk Lona said to Fran. Yeah, bring Elicia and Ann too.

They've GOTTA hear this! We're sticking together on this one!"

Four guys and a couple of girls were talking close by:

"Man, I'm hatin' that math homework. No way I'm gonna do that. Who's got the answers? Ah come on, somebody must have done it. You know she gets really ripped about that. Great, she'll be complaining for days. Wonder if Jamal did it... Somebody go get his paper and call out the answers. Might as well get it down before we go in. She'll never know anyway. You don't have to do much to get it checked off."

Away from them, about six girls were double-jumping rope at the tail end of the sidewalk, chanting childhood rhymes as they went round and round, counting the jumps before somebody missed. Breathless and grinning, they were completely unaware of the discussions around them, lost in the reverie of an old elementary school diversion that still held both appeal and a bit of innocence:

"Cin...da...RELL...a, dressed in YELL...a, kissed a SNAKE, by misTAKE. How many DOCtors did it TAKE? One...Two...Three... Four..."

Near them, a teacher on bus duty grinned inside herself. "Wonder how many snakes those girls will kiss before it's all over?" The little twinge that followed didn't go unrecognized. Sometimes she felt like the busiest doctor in town.

Her eyes surveyed the bus lot and stopped at the boy who stood near the door by himself most mornings. She considered walking over and talking to him but was a little unsure. Frankly, kids could be hard to predict; sometimes they didn't mind hanging out with the teacher and sometimes it was a social death sentence. She thought about him for a little while, and so for a few minutes escaped the roar around her. Carl was quite a bit smaller than many of the boys in her class, and lots of the girls too for that matter. She'd tried to get a handle on his personal life, but it was difficult without bluntly prying. She suspected that his parents were busy people who worked a lot and depended on the school--and her-- to take care of things for him during the majority of the day. She'd gotten used to that and didn't really mind. There was actually an easy rhythm to it after a while, and it gave her a feeling of focus and purpose. She just wished the others in class would pay him more attention. They didn't pick on him or anything; they just didn't see him. He was quickly turning into one of those kids who lived in that gray area that every teacher worries about.

She was suddenly pulled back into the moment by a pair of arms and a tight squeeze from behind. "Guess who?" the voice giggled, and she turned around to find Rachel and a couple of her friends there.

"Oh hi, girls," she laughed. "You startled me."

"Yeah," they teased. "You were really out of it. What's up?"

She relaxed as she launched into a quick listing of everything but Carl. She grinned. A hug, a few more girl-giggles, a promising spring morning... Now that was the way to start a Monday.

Just who are these kids we teach? What a difficult question to answer! As illustrated in our opening schoolyard scenario, they are exciting and frustrating, amiable and belligerent, focused and confused...each one, each day. They are both complex young adults who can make valuable contributions to our society, and insecure children who still need positive attention and constant encouragement. They are, above all, a unique collection of individuals whom we are challenged to love, to respect, to educate in such a way as to ensure their success in a society that is changing so rapidly that even the most astute adults find it difficult to adapt. If their success is to happen, then a rich understanding of this age group is certainly critical to an adult's most basic strategies and decisions concerning them.

This chapter will focus, in part, on a broad understanding of one aspect of growth among young teens, their emotional development. The most complex years on the life span are those that surround young adolescence, for these ten to fifteen-year-olds enter this period of rapid development as children and emerge as young adults. These years showcase profound physical, intellectual, emotional, moral, and social growth unlike any other in life, and as a result young adolescents tend to carry an overwhelming amount of emotional baggage during this period. This, in turn, often manifests itself in poor decision-making skills and habits. Educators find that these poor decisions then dramatically impact the social and academic paths that young adults find open to them in later life. In short, inadequate decision-making strategies are often based on fluctuating emotions and they touch every facet of young people's development, including both their academic and social worlds. This can then clearly leave them at risk of a diminished quality of life in our demanding, quickly changing, and often unforgiving society.

More specifically, this chapter digs into the question, "Just who are these kids we teach?" and in doing so describes the emotional baggage that a sample of contemporary thirteen-year-old adolescents carries. It then examines the use of realistic fiction as a curriculum and instructional strategy that has proved successful for classroom teachers interested in channeling their students in healthy emotional, social, and academic directions. Finally, it concludes by offering suggestions that enable teachers to learn more about adolescent development from their most valuable primary source, their students.

2. So who are these kids we teach?

The past thirty years of research have yielded any number of lists and descriptors that are designed to answer this question. One of the more amusing includes the following characteristics, with which most adults would surely agree (Knowles & Brown, 2000, p.2):

- They eat all the time.
- Their music is too loud.
- They take social issues very seriously.
- They frequently exclaim, "You don't understand!"
- They cry a lot.
- They laugh a lot.
- They are sure that nobody has ever felt what they are feeling.
- They like hanging out at home and being with their parents.
- They hate hanging out at home and being with their parents.
- They have difficulty attending to something for more than a minute at a time.
- They are plagued with acne.
- They are seldom satisfied with the way they look.
- They are loyal to their friends.
- They talk about their friends behind their backs.
- They outgrow their clothes every few months.

- Their voices crack when they sing in mixed chorus.
- They want to be independent.
- They do not want to let go of their childhood.

It's interesting to note how many of these descriptors collide with emotional development, isn't it? If adolescents are worried about, perhaps even obsessed with, their physical appearance for example, then that feeling can result in a student who is hesitant to present information to the class or even hand back corrected homework assignments. If another is fearful of not understanding the material taught, then that student certainly won't volunteer to participate in class and may waste valuable academic time dreading the possibility. Mad at your girlfriend? Slighted by your boyfriend? Don't have anyone to date? Whether genuine causes for concern or unfounded perceptions, such social worries can again be grounded in emotional development and will dramatically impact the quality of learning that occurs in the classroom. As is obvious, it's very difficult to separate the physical from the cognitive, and the resulting emotional baggage from social development.

How do early adolescents describe their world? Let's go back to our opening scenario and pose that question to a few of our students. There's no problem in that request, for early adolescents love to talk! Give them a telephone, a captive audience, a relevant question to respond to, and most teenagers will rattle on much longer than you've probably got time for. What sifts out is a kaleidoscopic view of the adolescent world as they live it, and as we adults rarely see it. Just who are these kids we teach? Let's ask them.

Young adolescents, both male and female, agree that peer relationships are extremely important to them, and they acknowledge that they are generally powerless to resist them, whether good or bad. When approached, our early morning friends talked openly about their world, and when they did, social interactions and emotional filters surfaced in all conversations, on all topics, at all times. Though they spoke individually, their commonalties were obvious, their insecurities evident, their honesty raw.

A few of our friends, like those still at a double-jumping rope stage, enjoy and value their relationships as new and exciting treasures. These are the youngsters who are just beginning to look beyond their families for entertainment, advice, support, and companionship. Jennifer and Shareeka are two examples of this:

> "Friends influence me a lot. I think they make about half my decisions. When I see my friends doing something, I want to do the exact same thing. Because one reason is I like having a good time, and another one is that I like being with my friends." (Jennifer)

> "For me, 13 years of age is the best age, to me at least. My friends and I have never been as close as we are now. We talk about everything. Just like we are sisters or something. Also, I've opened up to different kinds of people since I've reached 13." (Shareeka)

Still others, like our girls with the boyfriend woes, are well beyond the basics of same-sex relationships, and are more focused on the heart throbs of romantic involvement. Both boys and girls reach a stage where their thoughts and conversations seem dominated by their sexual development or decision-making agendas. Tonya and Ray continue the story:

> "You want to do what your friends do. You don't want to disappoint your friends. I like my friends to be loyal, trusting, secretive, nice. I don't want one that will lie to me. I have this friend. She went with this boy. This other girl, her supposed to be friend, kissed her boyfriend. My friend heard about this and asked her if she did kiss him; tell her so she would know the truth. Her friend then told her that he kissed her but she didn't kiss him. Then she wrote her a note just now and said her lips didn't touch his. My friend is very mad. I think she might try to fight her when they get alone." (Tonya)

> "Sexual decisions are almost common to everyone because of the age of today. It's like a status sign. It says whether you're in the crowd or out, usual or unusual. At times it's peer pressure to do it as well, and if you do you brag and make it well known as many times as you do it..." (Ray)

Sometimes peer and parental influences mingle in these conversations, and we adults must think through them more than once to sort out the moral code that these teenagers are exploring. Lona and Melinda's conversations are good examples of this:

"I used to sneak out to go meet my boyfriend every so often. I'd spend approximately three hours with him, then come home. I never got caught. Then when I was dating someone at this school, I spent the night with his friend's sister and he spent the night with his friend, once on a Saturday night and once on a school night. It's easy to do stuff like this when your parents trust you so much. I never once felt guilt because I never went all the way with anyone. I still do these things depending on who I'm dating." (Lona)

"I was at an older friend's house and they were having a party. I was offered to take drugs. Everything was fine until then. A lot of my friends was doing it. I couldn't believe my friends would do something like this to me. It was very unlike them. Some friends, HUH? All of my friends know that I wouldn't ever do it. But I feel like I was being pressured to do something that I didn't want to do. It made me feel bad and I realized what kind of friends they were. I decided to leave. I called my mom to come pick me up." (Melinda)

School is, of course, the stage on which the majority of a child's life plays out, from early kindergarten through graduation. It is, therefore, the one topic on which everyone wants to speak, the one where everyone has an opinion. Our bus lot kids are no different from most. Their stories about school range from tales of unjustified demerits, boring curriculum, and parent conferences to scenarios surrounding teachers who touch their lives in positive and unforgettable ways. Let's listen in:

"I have found no weaknesses in my teacher except one. That is the ability to stop everyone's life and just take out the bad pieces." (Shondra)

"Education is something that I think is good in general, especially in America where people are guaranteed an education. It gives people who want to learn a chance. I do, however, think that there are people who don't belong in the school system but are there anyway. There are teachers who don't like kids and kids who don't like learning. I love to learn if I am learning something that is interesting to me. But the most interesting part of a class is the teacher. If a teacher isn't imaginative and doesn't make the class fun, then the class is going to be boring. I think teachers should be monitored more closely, and should be evaluated more carefully. I also think that students should be interviewed as to what they think about their teacher and that this should be considered in the teacher's evaluation." (Gabe)

"Education is a great thing, but too much emphasis is put on going to college. I think there is nothing wrong with someone not going to college. There are a lot of good jobs that don't need college educations." (Mike)

"High school in my eyes is scary. I don't know why. But my guess is that since my sister told me about people smoking and trying to get you to smoke and do drugs and other stuff you don't want to. I guess that's why I'm scared of high school. They've got lots of great courses that I'm going to enjoy. Their teachers I've heard are not that much involved with their students. That's one thing I don't like. One thing I know I'm really going to enjoy is the freedom. My sister tells me there is lots of freedom there." (Kenecia)

From the decisions they confront to the educational standards they expect, early adolescents teach us a great deal about their world, and these illustrations serve to underscore the need for improved decision-making skills among them. All too often these children engage in behaviors that result in life-altering consequences. In addition to those shared here, for example, each day about 3,000 American teens smoke their first cigarette. At the same time, more than half of the country's sixth, seventh, and eighth graders are overweight, while many other young adolescent girls tenaciously diet as the result of our nation's punishing obsession with thinness (California Middle Grades Task Force, 2001).

As is obvious, "...there is a crucial need to help adolescents at this early age to acquire...a basis for making informed, deliberate decisions..." (Carnegie Council, 1989, p.12). The research study that provided the basis for this chapter's suggestions (Jones, 1999) acknowledged and addressed this "crucial need" for enhanced decision making among young adolescents, particularly in their social arena where so many of these decisions with heavy consequences occur. Specifically, the study delved into adolescent decision-making as it was described by a group of seventh grade reading students. The results of the eight-week study focused on the ways in which a literature-based curriculum influenced these young adults' perceptions of the social decisions that they make now, and those that they may face in their remaining adolescent years.

In order to provide a framework for understanding the need for this curriculum, and its potential effectiveness in both the classroom and the adolescent's personal domain, three major areas were explored: social and emotional development and decision making among young adolescents in general, successful approaches to school curriculum for the ten- to fifteen-year-old, and finally, the use of realistic adolescent fiction as an intervention with this particular seventh grade class.

3. The backdrop

Unrehearsed dilemmas generated by sexual temptations, emotional insecurities influenced heavily by peers, a constant fluctuation between dependence and independence, and a desperate search for sophistication are all characteristics of the social and emotional world in which emerging adolescents live. It is this social and emotional domain that is most heavily influenced by the other areas of adolescent development, as peer acceptance and popularity often become synonymous with security and positive self-esteem. This quest for peer acceptance frequently governs the social decisions that students make.

Hillman (1991, p.6) defined this peer group as "a small single-sex similar age group," although he continued by noting that most teens belong to any number of groups rather than just one. This social structure is of primary importance to the emerging adolescent's psychological well-being. Further, well-liked adolescents tend to be "active, successful, and happier." Hillman concluded by reporting that these peers often govern present issues, such as social activities and behaviors, while parents still influence matters of future concerns; for example, career choice and financial aspirations. Unfortunately, it is this concern over present social issues that often results in unhealthy decisions, and these in turn greatly impact the boundaries of career choice, financial aspiration, and other future opportunities.

McEwin and Thomason (1989, p.5) corroborated the thought that social and emotional growth in the emerging teen is especially strong. Emotions often rocket between euphoric highs and depressive lows, particularly in such areas as jealousy, love, fear, anger, and anxiety. Although intense, these feelings are often quick to subside and are therefore "not as expensive personally as those found in late adolescence and adulthood." This dramatic stage of social and emotional development is often characterized by responses that are out of proportion to the event. For example, students may display intense feelings of shame and humiliation over the smallest of social situations (Wood & Hillman, 1992).

Several educators call for an inclusion of decision-making skills integrated into relevant curriculum, and they guarantee that the resulting lifestyle will involve a brighter future for our youth. They also acknowledge, however, that this is a topic rarely addressed in systems governed by standardized testing and rigid curriculum mandates, though learning about social decision-making, healthy emotional growth, and problem solving should be a developmental right of all children, and the curriculum should include systematic instruction in those skills (Elias & Tobias, 1990; Scales, 1990).

It would seem that these concerns could be merged and successfully addressed in every classroom setting for the ten- to fifteen-year-old learner, and this goal has indeed shaped much of North Carolina's Standard Course of Study (N.C. Department of Public Instruction, 1999). However, many classrooms continue to emphasize the obvious academic application of skills while ignoring the impact that an adolescent's social world and personal experiences have on scholastic success. Therefore, an incorporation of social decision making into a literacy curriculum could increase the opportunities for a young adolescent's future success by merging relevant life experiences and curriculum mandates.

4. Using realistic fiction to enhance social decision making

Realistic Fiction

Realistic fiction introduces the young adolescent to both high-level social decision making and the lure of relevant print. It is consuming and empowering. Within the pages of a contemporary novel, the student finds a world that provides room and board to other young adolescents who face similar problems and who must also make stressful choices. In realistic fiction, the student meets characters who too face escalated periods of personal development, the popularity of alcohol and tobacco use among parents and friends, decisions concerning sexual participation, the increased pressure for peer conformity, changing family agendas... and always, a heightened sense of confusion over the complexities of it all.

Middle school students are often reluctant readers, and realistic fiction offers a solution to this situation, as well as to the need for increased participation in decision-making scenarios. Early adolescents embrace this genre for a variety of reasons, and primarily because it is written specifically for their age group, is easily read and well written, and does not resemble a traditional textbook.

Issacs (1992, p. 139) suggested that teachers would do well to pay careful attention to the titles and authors that their students select, and to use some of their choices in the classroom's curriculum, for "Peer relationships are vitally important in the middle school years and these students, like any middle school students, depend much more on each other than on adults for reading recommendations."

Becoming a Nation of Readers: The Report of the Commission on Reading (Anderson, Hiebert, Scott, & Wilkinson, 1985, pp. 117-120) quickly became a landmark report in America, and it offered suggestions that are still relevant to the problem of classroom curriculum today. Specifically, it recommended that:

(1) Teachers must create a classroom environment that is literate, stimulating, and well-disciplined, with "an adequate amount of time allocated to reading and writing."
(2) Teachers must fully attend to comprehension instruction in the classroom.

(3) The use of workbooks and skills sheets should be closely monitored. They monopolize time in the classroom, "despite the fact that there is little evidence that these activities are related to reading achievement."

(4) Independent reading, both at school and outside of the classroom, should be promoted. It is directly correlated with an increase in reading achievement.

(5) Children should be offered frequent opportunities to write, for this too impacts reading ability.

(6) Schools should cultivate a reading atmosphere that permeates everything.

(7) The school library should be recognized as a key component in this "becoming a nation of readers." Libraries should therefore be well-stocked and appropriately staffed.

Both the invitation to read and the call to examine characters under safe conditions must be recognized and addressed by educators of adolescents. The Carnegie Council (1989, p. 29) warned that ill-prepared young adults "...with minimal competencies will barely get by. The most poorly prepared will move in and out of crime, drug abuse, or alcoholism." The Council's challenge is clear. The best classrooms at the middle level are those where instruction is relevant, child-centered, and integrated. Reading realistic fiction with students gives teachers an opportunity to initiate the practices seen in the classrooms of the best teachers while offering these complex young adolescents an opportunity to safely discover the habits associated with healthy decision making.

An overview of the study that merged realistic fiction and decision making

Grounded in 31 examples of realistic fiction, this eight-week curriculum invited a class of seventh grade students into the world of print, where they discovered a host of characters who lived the same confusions, struggled with the same dilemmas, and resolved the same conflicts as those that they had reported earlier in journal entries and on questionnaires. As a result, these students found a literary peer group that was immersed in developmental diversities and social decision-making situations. In short, these books provided a mirror image of the world in which these students lived.

This study relied on the DECIDE model (Durrant, Frey, & Newbury, 1991) for the decision-making framework. This particular model was selected because it featured a simple acronym and was easy to memorize, thus enhancing the probability that it would become intrinsic to the lives of the study's participants. The curriculum designed for the study nurtured an understanding of this model as it applied first to the book selections and then to the students' personal worlds. The following is the DECIDE model as it was presented to and practiced by the students:

Describe the problem.
Explore to identify solutions.
Consider the consequences of each solution.
Identify the best solution.
Do it.
Evaluate your decision and learn from it.

Once both novels and a decision-making model had been selected, the question of daily curriculum was addressed. The North Carolina English Language Arts competency-based Standard Course of Study was reviewed for grade 7. This also pulled back into play the research on successful middle grades curriculum, which called for such things as "...a curriculum of and for the young adolescent...a curriculum which embraces and addresses the social meanings sought by them and...members of the school community" (McDonough, 1991, p. 29). Therefore, both the state curriculum guide and the national movement for improved middle grades curriculum and instruction supplied a framework for curriculum design. In addition, emphasis was placed on keeping each day's instruction interesting and relevant, with the DECIDE model supplying a common point of focus for the 31 novels, which were primarily read through an approach commonly known as literature circles. This particular strategy was used because it allowed the students to freely choose among the available novels and to initiate their own discussions of them.

For example, two novels were initially taught one at a time to the entire class. This allowed for the introduction of the decision-making model in the first book and a deeper understanding of its applicability to the characters through the second. After this was done, students were given the opportunity to read two additional novels of their choosing from among the selected titles, with these being taught through the small literature circles. Guided questions ensured common ground among these circles of discussants. Once a full understanding of the decision-making model and its application was ensured, the entire class read a final and fifth novel together, which provided an application of the model to the students' personal lives.

As the study progressed, information applicable to both decision-making concerns and the adolescents' social world was gathered from the 28 seventh graders and their reading teacher. This was accomplished through a variety of data collection instruments including, among others: questionnaires, reader response journals, and formal writing assignments. Additionally, seven students were interviewed on several occasions to clarify the class voice. All students' responses concerning their world were rich in detail, often unsolicited, and compellingly honest.

The results of this data collection were analyzed qualitatively according to the guidelines suggested by Lincoln and Guba (1985), including a triangulation of data. In doing so, emerging frames of reference were consistently fine-tuned until a full understanding of all perceptions became evident. All conclusions were shared with and corroborated by the classroom teacher, the students and their families.

On a closing note, the North Carolina Standard Course of Study and components of solid middle school curriculum were regarded at all times. Specifically:

- Diverse levels of student development were respected; for example, maturity and interest levels, and reading and writing abilities.
- Good communication skills were stressed at all times, primarily: listening, speaking, reading, writing, and viewing.
- Academic achievement and engagement with the learning process were emphasized.
- Skills sheets, workbooks, and rote application of teacher's manuals were all avoided.
- Motivational strategies were kept at a premium; for example, the use of trade books, book talks, group work, unstructured class discussions, and enthusiasm.

- Basal textbooks were abandoned for the more natural language and relevant situations common to trade books.
- Diverse characteristics of developing adolescents were replicated by characters within the book selections; therefore, an enhanced understanding of self was nurtured within each student.
- Reading was accomplished in a variety of ways so as to strengthen basic skills: oral reading by the instructor and student volunteers, group reading both aloud and silently, and independent reading outside of the classroom.
- Cultural differences were noted within the novels. These differences were then correlated to the students' own lives, promoting respect for others and tolerance of the individualities of others.
- Relevant decision-making situations were portrayed in each of the trade books read. The DECIDE model, an example of a planned approach, was used as the key for examination because it could be easily understood by the diverse levels found within this classroom. The model was applied often to the literature, ensuring comprehension. Only then could it be transferred into the lives of the individual students.
- The media center was utilized and promoted (both school and city).
- Parents were interested and involved.
- Finally, the Carnegie Council's (1989, p.15) vision of the healthy young adolescent was associated with all aspects of the learning process. This child was noted as one who is "...an intellectually reflective person, a person enroute to a lifetime of meaningful work, a good citizen, a caring and ethical individual, and a healthy person."

Results

These students emerged as an array of young adolescents who regularly face challenging social situations. Initiation into their world can be found in their responses to the opening questionnaire's prompt: "Think back to a time when you faced a difficult choice or temptation, one that involved other people in a social setting (including school). Describe the setting where you were, and then describe the situation in detail, including how you felt."

Eager to discuss their social life, these students shared a kaleidoscopic view of the adolescent world as they lived it, and which we have now shared through their voices in the opening pages of this chapter. They were at all times highly cognizant of their peer relationships; they acknowledged that these were both positive and negative, and that they were generally powerless to resist them. These interactions and influences surfaced in all conversations, on all topics, at all times, and they were obviously charged with emotional investment.

In the closing days of the study, students described a medley of situations and dilemmas, agendas and phases, strategies and struggles. They came to understand, in varying degrees, that social situations affect everyone, and that each person has the responsibility to both recognize and address them in a mature and controlled fashion. One endorsement of this growing awareness was found in a comparison of the entire group's initial and closing questionnaires. Eighty-nine percent referenced some aspect of a systematic approach to decision making in the first questionnaire, and ninety-three percent referenced one in the closing. Although this degree of growth does not seem particularly significant, it is when reviewed in light of recognized consequences. The majority of students in this class began to realize that decisions often have long-term effects and that these must be carefully considered as part of the decision-making process; therefore, it is not simply good enough to think through a decision in terms of "Will I?" or "Won't I?" Rather, one must consider the ramifications of each possible option. This realization accounted for a dramatic shift away from choices made for immediate gratification and toward those that recognized short- and long-term effects. Table 1 highlights a comparison of the opening and closing questionnaires in this area.

Table 1
Percentage of students' initial and final response by categories of response ($n= 28$)

Category	Initial responses	Final responses
Made a choice involving immediate gratification	40	10
Made a choice involving short-range consequences	44	75
Made a choice involving long-range consequences	8	10
Made a choice involving a mixture of short and long-range consequences	8	5

The possible impact of realistic adolescent fiction on personal lives

The DECIDE model provided a vehicle for students to use when analyzing the decisions found within the stories introduced in class. It was therefore important for them to frequently apply a personal understanding of this model to adolescent fiction in whatever way was appropriate for each individual's developmental level. This recurrent and effective application ensured both an understanding of a systematic approach to decision making and an internalizing of the steps involved, which would lead students to a spontaneous application of it in private.

In unsolicited journal entries, 24 of the 28 students in this class, or 86%, noted that realistic fiction could be a basis for consultation when difficult decisions arise. For example:

> "Some books can have an effect on people. For example, if you are having trouble at home… your parents are fussing at you every day. You decide you would run away. You could read a book about someone running away and quitting school. You will know what kind of future they've got. You might see what would happen to you. That might have been a fiction book, but it could have been written just for you. You might change your mind and think more about what you were going to do." (Sara)

> "I think literature has a lot to do with decisions. The books that we're reading have seemed so real. You can look back at the books and see that their decisions are very much like ours. If you ever have a problem or a decision to make, you can look back at the books if they are similar to yours." (Melinda)

> "You can learn from the mistakes these characters make in their decisions." (Scottie)

These students enjoyed the curriculum that was introduced into both their reading classroom and their lives, for it provided them with a vehicle into a literary world that was a mirror image of their own. Immersed in this new environment, they found themselves free to safely explore and experiment with characters and circumstances that were common to their own lives. In the majority, it awakened a sense of greater control over their social world and provided a systematic approach to decision making within it.

5. Conclusions

In order to truly reflect on the questions "Who are these kids we teach?" and "How can we contribute to their healthy development?", it is imperative that we continue to research our particular students. True, classroom observations and assessments will share their intellectual development, but these same procedures will not tell us much about their social and emotional growth, and their decision-making skills. Fortunately, there are several interesting ways to add these dimensions to our personal perspectives. For example:

- Continue to read contemporary adolescent fiction with an eye turned to emotional development and social decision making. These books reflect the world in which your students live, a world that otherwise remains closed to you by virtue of your adult status.
- Spend at least 30 minutes observing early--and older--adolescents at a popular hangout aside from school; for example, outside the entrance to a local game room or movie theatre, or in any area where teens spend their free time. Watch objectively for maturity levels, social interactions, and decision making.
- Distribute index cards in class occasionally and ask your students to jot down their opinions, concerns, and questions on a variety of topics. Select these prompts, sentence starters, or scenarios based on personal interests or prior classroom events and conversations. These might include such things as: How important is education in your life? Describe your favorite teacher. What's it like to be ___ years old? or What's the hardest decision you've ever had to make? Anonymity tends to ensure honesty.
- Ask your students to bring their favorite magazines to class or ask them to provide you with a list of those titles. Thoroughly examine them from a clinical perspective, including articles, advertisements, and photography. What do your kids learn about themselves and our society from those periodicals? Once you've drawn your conclusions, design a reading lesson around the same questions and compare your opinions with your students'.

- Survey your students as to their favorite television shows and encourage them to keep a "Viewer's Log" of the amount of time they watch TV in one week. Watch the shows that are most popular with them and ask yourself again, "What do my students learn about themselves and our society from these programs?" Design a lesson around this event as well, and then compare your opinions with your students'.

And what can we expect to learn from these observations and conversations? Our students will probably show us that the old adage is true: The more things look different, the more they're really the same. You will surely find that your children are like people of all ages everywhere, with basic needs and desires. You will also learn that, like all of us, they harbor simple dreams of successful futures where they're good parents and good workers making a solid contribution to the future of their country. Talk to them; they'll open your eyes to an entire world of possibilities.

References

Anderson, R.C., Hiebert, E.H., Scott, J.A., & Wilkinson, I.A.G. (1985). *Becoming a nation of readers: The report of the Commission on Reading*. Washington, DC: The National Institute of Education.

Carnegie Council on Adolescent Development. (1989). *Turning points: Preparing American youth for the 21st century*. NY: Carnegie Corporation.

Durrant, L., Frey, D., & Newbury, K. (1991). Discover skills for life. San Diego, CA: Educational Assessment Publishing Co.

Elias, M.J., & Tobias, S.E. (1990). *Problem solving / decision making for social and academic success*. Washington, DC: National Education Association.

George, P.S. (1991). Student development and middle level school organization: A prolegomenon. Midpoints: *Occasional papers, 1*. Columbus, OH: National Middle School Association.

Hillman, S.B. (1991). What developmental psychology has to say about early adolescence? *Middle School Journal, 23*, 3-8.

Isaacs, K.T. (1992). Go ask Alice: What middle schoolers choose to read. *The New Advocate, 5*, 129-144.

Jones, J.P. (1999). Embracing the 21st century: Healthy lifestyles for young adolescents. In M.L. Calhoun & H. Melenk (Eds.), *Students at risk: Educational strategies in the United States and in Germany*. Charlotte, NC: University of NC at Charlotte.

Knowles, T., & Brown, D. (2000). *What every middle school teacher should know*. Portsmouth, NH: Heineman.

Lincoln, Y.S., & Guba, E.G. (1985). *Naturalistic inquiry.* Beverly Hills, CA: Sage Publications.

McDonough, L. (1991). Middle level curriculum: The search for self and social meaning. *Middle School Journal, 23,* 29-35.

McEwin, K., & Thomason, J. (1989). *Who they are? How we teach: Early adolescents and their teachers.* OH: National Middle School Association.

Middle Grades Task Force. (2001). *Taking center stage: A commitment to standards-based education for California's middle grades students.* Sacramento, CA: California Department of Education.

North Carolina Department of Public Instruction. (1999). *English language arts standard course of study.* Raleigh, NC: NCDPI. (www.ncpublicschools.org/curriculum/languagearts/)

Scales, P. (1990). Developing capable young people: An alternative strategy for prevention programs. *Journal of Early Adolescence, 10,* 420-438.

Wood, P.C., & Hillman, S.B. (1992). Developmental issues of very young adolescents. *Middle School Journal, 23,* 14-19.

CHAPTER 7

The role of anxiety in metacognition in mathematics

Louise Lafortune and Francisco Pons

1. Introduction

Many students drop or fail math courses within the course of their education. Even as adults many can remember learning situations in mathematics that have left them with mental scars (Lafortune, 1990, 1992a-b; Tobias, 1978, 1987). Difficult and negative prior experiences influence the way children tackle and try to solve mathematical problems. Certain people are convinced they cannot succeed in mathematics, while others do all they can to avoid any situation in which they might encounter mathematical problems. These situations may result in an aversion to mathematics (Kogelman & Warren, 1978; Lafortune, 1992a-b; Martinez & Martinez, 1996; Tobias, 1978, 1987; Zaslavsky, 1994). Many students are incapable of devoting the necessary attention and readily give up looking for solutions to mathematical problems (Lafortune, 1995). Their negative emotional reactions to mathematics interfere with their metacognitive knowledge and processes; therefore they also interfere with their abilities to learn mathematics and to use their mathematics knowledge (Lafortune & St-Pierre, 1994a-b). Based on these findings, we aim to study the effect of emotional reactions on the metacognitive processes in students trying to solve mathematical problems.

As a component of the emotional domain, anxiety has not been fully explored in relation to metacognition in mathematics. Since the 1970s the emotional domain has given rise to more research involving how people learn mathematics, and it appears to be a factor influencing the pleasure of learning mathematics (Kogelman & Warren, 1978; Lafortune, 1990, 1992a-b, 1995; Lafortune, Mongeau, Daniel & Pallascio, 2000; Martinez

& Martinez, 1996; Nimier, 1976, 1988; Tobias, 1978, 1987, 1990; Weyl-Kailey, 1985; Zaslavsky, 1994). Mathematics can be successfully learned despite the accompanying anxiety; however, the pleasure and enjoyment of learning may be affected (MEQ, 2001).

This chapter will focus primarily on anxiety regarding mathematics and its influence on the mental processes of students. It will outline the problem of math anxiety by examining those aspects related to teaching and those related to learning. We will provide a definition of mathematics anxiety and also briefly explain what is meant by "metacognition". This will establish a link between metacognition, emotional reaction, and more precisely, anxiety. We shall conclude by making proposals for research which we believe stems from research conducted with regard to issues of anxiety and metacognition in mathematics.

2. Mathematics anxiety: The problem

Since the beginning of the 1970s researchers and educators have been concerned about the emotional dimension resulting from difficulties experienced by students in mathematics. Among the components of this dimension, anxiety was the first to arouse interest. Since then, several authors have become interested in this topic (Hatchuel, 2000; Kogelman & Warren, 1978; Lafortune, 1990, 1992b, 1995; Lafortune, Mongeau, Daniel & Pallascio, 2000; Martinez & Martinez, 1996; Nimier, 1976, 1985; Tobias, 1978, 1987, 1990; Weyl-Kailey, 1985; Zaslavsky, 1994). For some persons, mathematics is a nightmare. Others have the impression that when mathematics is explained to them, a veil (or even a wall) is erected before them. This wall blocks the concentration they require to understand what is being explained. Therefore, mathematics becomes a painful experience which can lead such persons to choose their scholastic path according to the number of mathematics courses required (Wigfield & Meece, 1988, quoted in Meece, Wigfield & Eccles, 1990).

Earlier research enabled us to unearth some of the reasons that cause learners to develop negative emotional reactions to mathematics. Even though we are aware that these reasons extend beyond the school environment, we will focus more particularly on those that relate to teaching and learning.

Response to the teaching of mathematics

In the teaching of mathematics a great deal of attention is paid to the syllabus. This emphasis on the content of teaching programs often prevents teachers from devoting time to the attitudes and emotional reactions of learners towards mathematics. The emotional dimension in learning is often considered as additional work and perceived as a waste of time: 1) Even if the school environment recognizes the importance of intervening at the emotional level for mathematics students, soon arguments emphasizing "actual teaching" take center stage. 2) As the cognitive dimension becomes paramount, learners begin to realize that it is normal to feel anxiety about mathematics, feel helpless whenever they are uncomfortable in a problem-solving situation and begin to avoid situations involving mathematics. 3) It may be assumed that by implementing the spirit of the new program in Quebec schools, the negative effect resulting from too great an emphasis on content, to the detriment of positive attitudes towards the discipline, will be diminished.

Some teachers' conception of mathematics is too restricted. At the primary level, arithmetic is given too much importance to the detriment of geometry. This situation leads the students to believe that "real math" relates to calculation, and that "geometry" is not mathematics (Lafortune, 1994). Some students who obtain good grades in geometry receive no recognition for their success. The difficulties they are experiencing in arithmetic result in an overall feeling of thinking they are not good in mathematics. In such a context, it is very difficult to make intra-disciplinary links in class. Even though the use of geometry and arithmetic is required in many problem-solving situations, the elements of mathematics are viewed as separate entities.

Some primary school teachers, themselves, have a negative attitude towards mathematics. Mathematics is not their preferred subject and they are hesitant to step outside of the strict syllabus guidelines, because they do not feel comfortable with the discipline. Their limited knowledge and background in relation to mathematics leads them to present mathematics in its algorithmic, technical and procedural dimensions. Therefore, they create a situation which does not encourage students to develop their own intuition and creativity in mathematics. In addition, such a situation severely limits critical thinking. Those students who are not at ease with this approach lose interest in mathematics which can result in a loss of mathematical creativity, thereby creating negative reactions to mathematics.

These negative attitudes towards mathematics are compounded by a certain reticence towards using metacognitive, reflective or innovative approaches. Arguments used often center on the time spent on various activities with learners which do not relate specifically to the mathematics syllabus. This situation shows a certain reticence towards innovation, either because of insecurity with regard to changing habits, or through a lack of information and teacher training in the use of new methodologies, especially in mathematics. Some traditional methods of teaching mathematics often lead to thinking that "doing mathematics" implies memorizing procedures, applying them and finding solutions. Within this context, learners who use different methods from those taught can be penalized although their way of solving problems might be in keeping with relevant or heuristic processes in mathematics. If they are never made aware of the links, they might conclude that they do not have what they refer to as "mathematical logic."

Reactions linked to learning mathematics

Several learners have gaps in the knowledge required to effectively learn mathematics. This may be due to difficulty in concentrating, difficulty in making the effort required to integrate the knowledge, problems of comprehension or family concerns. These gaps and difficulties prevent some learners from listening attentively and participating fully in math activities. As a result, there is an ever-widening gap between these learners and others in the class. This gap causes students to feel they will never be able to make up for lost time. This lack of basic knowledge combined with individual learning problems may lead to repeated failure which discourage the learners and sap their perseverance.

Baruk (1973, 1977, 1985) has carried out extensive research on the meaning these children attach to mathematical statements. She demonstrates that how mathematical statements are formulated or presented can confuse children (Baruk, 1989). For example, if students are asked, "which is bigger: two elephants or eight carrots?" they are in fact being asked to compare items that are not comparable. Moreover, for a child, two elephants are bigger than eight carrots in the physical sense of the term. However, if it is the number of objects being referred to, then the child will be expected to answer "eight carrots". This example may seem ridiculous but if we examine what the students are being asked or ask them why they gave a particular answer, we will realize that their interpretations make sense and should be taken into consideration. Baruk (1977) also shows how the students interpret comments, often indicated by symbols that are written on their scripts. For example, an error of calculation which seems clear to the teacher, is indicated by a large "X" or by a question mark "?" or by the comment "Really!" often written in red. These symbols have little meaning for the students and force them to interpret their errors. The students develop a new way of doing things which worsens a simple error of calculation (Baruk, 1977). Over time, this (calculation) error which could have been easily corrected, becomes a "horrible error" (reasoning error).

Mathematics is a discipline involving several types of language: natural, symbolic and graphic. De Serres and Groleau (1977) developed an instrument to deal more effectively with the poor grades some of the mathematics students obtained because of their language difficulties. Even though their work was carried out at the college level, the results shed light on the difficulties encountered by learners in mathematics at the primary level. The fact that mathematics requires translation skills is often ignored. For example, a statement expressed in natural language often requires graphical representation, such as, transference into symbolic mathematical language to solve the problem and then transference back into natural language to better present the solution to the problem. To ignore this particular situation in mathematics and science is to disregard some of the difficulties being encountered by learners. St-Hilaire (1989) points out the traumatizing impact of this mathematical language. She could not imagine that a letter of the alphabet could be squared. To counter this difficulty, during a statistics course she re-wrote all her course notes by transferring each formula into natural language in order to grasp its meaning. *She writes it is this act of "translation into French" which allowed [me] to understand these formulae by placing them within [my] reach.* This example is similar to those given by Tobias (1987) who states that several adults translate in order to understand mathematics.

Learners themselves also harbor beliefs and prejudices with regard to mathematics, the learning of mathematics and the persons who teach it.

Lafortune (1994) documented the beliefs and prejudices expressed by learners in the very terms they used. For example, the following statements were documented: "Mathematics is nothing more than arithmetic; mathematics is like magic; to be a whiz in math is to be boring; it means "sucking up to" the teacher and "math teachers are dull". These beliefs and prejudices cause students enrolling in a mathematics course to believe that the course will be boring and that success in geometry is less important than in arithmetic or algebra. They cause them to denigrate those students who are doing well and to think that success is linked to the possession of some sort of special or superior talent. This latter belief leads some learners to justify their failures. It gives them a pretext for dropping math when the course becomes difficult because they think they do not have a good head for mathematics (see also Lafortune, Mongeau & Pallascio, 2000). However, Dehaene (1997) defends the theory that if such a thing as a "good head for math" exists, then everybody has one. Citing the work of other researchers, Lucangeli and Cornoldi (1999) point out the three fundamental beliefs outlined by Schoenfeld (1987). First, mathematics has no basis in reality. Second, mathematical problems are solved in less than ten minutes or otherwise cannot be solved. Third, only geniuses are able to discover or create mathematics. They also cite Scommer, Grouse and Rhodes (1992) who refer to four fundamental beliefs. First, the ability to learn mathematics is an innate one. Second, learning is easy and based on speed. Third, knowledge of mathematics is clear and unambiguous. Forth, knowledge of mathematics is free of uncertainties and represents the truth. Zaslavsky (1996) also cites beliefs which are propagated with regard to mathematics and the learning of this discipline. Beliefs such as "mathematics is for boys; men have more spatial skills than women which makes them superior; Asians are superior to other cultural groups with regard to mathematics; and Whites are intellectually superior to Blacks" are supported in his work. These beliefs and prejudices affect the attitude which students take into mathematics courses. It is difficult to eradicate such attitudes within a short period of time. However, it is important to make young persons reflect on these beliefs very early in their school life.

Several authors have examined the situation of negative attitudes with regard to mathematics (Anthony, 1996; Baruk, 1973, 1985; Enemark & Wise, 1981, in Ma & Kishor, 1997; Fennema & Sherman, 1976; Goos

& Galbraith, 1996; Jitendra & Xin, 1997; Lafortune, 1987, 1988, 1990, 1992a-b; Lafortune, Mongeau, Daniel & Pallascio, 2000; McLeod, 1994; Meravech & Kramarski, 1997; Nimier, 1976, 1985; Petit & Zawojwoski, 1997; Tobias, 1978, 1987). These negative attitudes may be linked to self-esteem, emotional response (anxiety, commitment and pleasure), beliefs and prejudices or attributional control beliefs (Lafortune, Mongeau, Daniel & Pallascio, 2000; 2002a-b). This team of researchers established a link between the various components of these attitudes. It is in fact difficult to determine which of these components of attitude intervenes first in the negative reactions of the students.

Is it anxiety with regard to mathematics that influences self-esteem where this discipline is concerned or vice-versa? In several studies she conducted, Lafortune (1988, 1990, 1992a-b) developed a hypothesis regarding the interactions between the various components of negative emotional reactions of students to mathematics. According to this hypothesis, several prior experiences may lead students to adopt negative attitudes towards mathematics. Prior experiences such as repeated failure, a negative attitude on the part of the teacher, confusion between the different meanings given to mathematical statements or lack of prior knowledge. These experiences may become traumatizing and may create anxiety with regard to mathematics which in turn may lead to withdrawal or aversion.

3. Mathematics anxiety: Different emotional reactions

Math anxiety is manifested in various ways. In research conducted with adults enrolled in a mathematics course, Lafortune (1992a-b) identified many forms of anxiety (worry, uneasiness and even fear). **Worry** is manifested through a student's preoccupation with the manner in which a course will be conducted. Because of apprehensions, he or she appears to have a negative attitude even before starting the course or engaging in any mathematical activity. This worry is triggered by past experiences or beliefs and misconceptions about the difficulty of mathematics, such as its uselessness or the conviction that only a chosen few with superior talent can master mathematics. These are popular misconceptions propagated by both school and society. **Uneasiness** about mathematics creates tension in students which is sometimes difficult to cope with. It also causes them to keep mathematical activity to a minimum. Uneasiness usually surfaces when a student attempts to solve mathematical problems or when he or she recalls previous difficulties. **Fear** has more far-reaching effects; it causes avoidance. In this case, only specific and sustained intervention can rectify these negative perceptions.

Does anxiety always have a negative impact on mathematics learning? Several research findings (Fasko & Skidmore, 1999; Lafortune, Mongeau, Daniel & Pallascio, 2002a-b; McInerney, McInerney & Marsh, 1997) have led us to question the purely negative influence of anxiety with regard to the learning of mathematics. In their findings, McInerney, McInerney and Marsh (1997) suggest that anxiety may even facilitate learning for some students. By studying anxiety with regard to computers and comparing two pedagogical strategies (direct instruction to a large group and collaborative learning related to metacognitive strategies), this team of researchers determined there was decreased anxiety among the most anxious university students in which direct learning was favored, rather than in the group where a more innovative approach was adopted. Looking at the school performance, Naveh, Benjamin, McKeachie and Lin (1987), Tobias (1986) and Wigfield and Eccles (1989) noted that anxiety did not always have a negative effect on school performance. Moreover, it seems that girls experience more anxiety than boys in mathematics (Fasko & Skidmore, 1999; Lafortune, Mongeau, Daniel & Pallascio, (2002a), Marsh, 1988, quoted in Viau, 1995); however, their results in mathematics are very similar (MEQ, 2001). This raises the question as to whether this anxiety is as damaging as has always been suggested.

All these findings have led us to support the view that math anxiety is an emotional state with two facets. It may be an emotional state characterized by worry, uneasiness and fear that may impede the ability to do mathematics. On the other hand, this emotional state also has a positive dimension. It is characterized by excitement and the desire to rise to a challenge which results in pride and even pleasure in doing mathematics. Relatively intense emotions (positive or negative) also hamper concentration and the ability to perform to one's full capacity.

According to Morris, Davis and Hutchins (1981), quoted by Fasko and Skidmore, (1999), the cognitive component is influenced by personal evaluation of the situation in relation to one's previous experiences. This second component is, by nature, well thought-out while the emotional component is short-lived and is not based on an evaluation of the context. For example, anxiety may be attributed more to class organization than to any personal inner reaction associated with past experiences.

In current research that is nearing completion[1], we studied mathematics anxiety in children 9 to 12 years of age. A philosophical approach to mathematics was used. (Lafortune, Mongrau, Daniel & Pallascio, 2002a-b). Without presenting this study in its entirety, we shall discuss some of the findings relating to differences between girls and boys with respect to the expression of their anxiety towards this discipline.

Girls seem to feel and express internal anxiety towards mathematics. For example, they may say: "I think I'm losing self control; I'm beginning to feel nervous: I don't know what to do; I don't know where to start." The following comments exemplify the same thinking pattern: "I feel so tense that I'm unable to do anything; I'm shaking all over; I can't even think about mathematics any more, all I want is the answer, the answer, the answer".

Boys, on the other hand, often give external reasons for not being able to solve math problems. When they have difficulties, it is sometimes expressed under the guise of frustrations mainly due to the reactions of others. For example, if others understand, boys may say: "This problem was child's play; I'm not intelligent enough; I feel bad." What others think is important for boys. Other boys will say, "sometimes when doing a problem, I feel I'm wasting my time; [then] I'll try another problem." Others add, "I don't usually feel tense about problems. I'm not easily disturbed. If a problem disturbs me, I just don't do it."

When we see these avoidance reactions in boys, we may come to the conclusion that it might be preferable to feel a level of anxiety towards mathematics. We also conclude that alternative approaches might exist (reflexive, metacognitive or philosophical) to question the beliefs and biases of girls towards mathematics if, after a period of disequilibrium, the state of anxiety can be turned into a state of excitement.

It should be noted that neither the reaction of girls (intrinsic anxiety) nor that of boys (external reasons for their difficulties) leads to pleasure in doing mathematics. We may even link these findings to those of the third international survey on mathematics and sciences carried out in

1999 (MEQ, 2001). These findings reveal that in Quebec, girls have as much success in mathematics as boys, and Quebec youngsters obtain the best results in all of Canada. However, of all the Canadian provinces, students of both sexes in Quebec least enjoy learning mathematics. It is therefore easy to conclude that dislike for mathematics does not really affect scholastic results. However, this situation can lead to avoidance of careers in the sciences. The scarcity of professionals in the fields of science and technology in Quebec could be attributable to the minimal pleasure derived from learning mathematics and perhaps to excessive anxiety in some persons or indifference on the part of others (Tousignant, 1999).

Although several cognitive aspects may be linked to these emotional reactions, we will look specifically at what relates to metacognition.

4. Metacognition

Metacognition refers to the attention a person pays to his or her mental processes with a view to planning, evaluating, adjusting, and verifying his or her own learning process. There are three associated components: metacognitive knowledge, thought process management, and awareness of mental processes. These three components lead to the development of metacognitive skills. Metacognitive knowledge is knowledge and beliefs about cognition-related phenomena. This may relate to a persons (knowing one's strengths and weaknesses and comparing them to those of others) tasks (determining whether a problem is easy or difficult to solve), or strategies for their performance (what to use, time and manner of use).

Thought process management refers to the processes that a person sets in motion to control and manage his or her own thinking. These include planning (anticipating the result), monitoring (evaluating mental processes as they take place), and regulation (adjusting strategies in response to this evaluation). Thought process management is more difficult to verbalize and depends on the type of problem to be solved and the context involved (see Brown, 1987; Doudin & Martin, 1992; Flavell, 1979, 1987; Lafortune, 1998, Lafortune & St-Pierre, 1994a-b, 1996; Martin, Doudin & Albanese, 2001).

Awareness of one's thought processes enhances metacognitive knowledge and influences mental activity during problem solving. The conscious nature of metacognition assumes great importance in its development (Pons & Harris, 2001; Pons, Doudin, Martin, Lafortune & Harris, 2004), particularly in the learning situation (Lafortune & St-Pierre, 1994a-b, 1996). It facilitates improved verbalization of thought processes which in turn improves the quality of communication with others. The aspect of communication is aimed at understanding one's own reactions (realizing that one is not alone in experiencing math anxiety), and improving performance (making use of strategies devised by others to improve the approach to problem solving).

5. Metacognition and emotional responses

In examining the link between motivation and metacognition, Carr (1996) refers to studies on motivation, social influences and cognitive and metacognitive development. She notes that these factors have each been studied by various researchers but that very few – she names none – have looked at the interaction between these elements in connection with performance in mathematics. Fasko and Skidmore (1999) make a similar observation. According to Carr (1996), the difference between boys and girls merits special attention. More specifically, she suggests that research should focus on parents' beliefs, pointing out that they have different ideas about the ability of boys and girls to do mathematics. She notes in her work that as students become more advanced in their academic careers, the link between their motivation and level of metacognitive skill and their results in mathematics becomes stronger. This observation supports the results of the meta-analysis done by Ma and Kishor (1997). Some aspects of the research by Carr (1996) focus on the role of emotional response in metacognition in mathematics. She points out that when students are facing new situations in which they must question their usual ways of thinking and acting, they may be disturbed. According to her, this disturbed feeling arises when a student, while using a familiar problem-solving technique, encounters an obstacle or gets an unexpected result (for example too large a number or a strange fraction). There are three likely reactions to these feelings: the student may show indifference and move on to the next problem; she or he may re-evaluate the processes involved or attempt a new and different approach; or they may modify or adapt their individual approach. Disturbance may occur at the conscious or unconscious level. If one believes that to be disturbed is to be off balance, troubled or overwhelmed, one may conclude that this could lead to anxiety defined as an emotional state giving rise to worry, uneasiness or fear.

Without making direct reference to mathematics, Wilson and Brekke (1994) cited in Wilson, Gilbert and Wheatley (1998) point to the role of emotion and belief in metacognition. With regard to emotion, they refer to 'mental contamination'. It is defined as a process in which, as a result of unconscious or uncontrollable thought processes, involuntary judgments, or emotions or behaviors arise. To facilitate metacognitive development, the authors emphasize the importance of having enough control of one's thought process to avoid the disturbance associated with the 'mental contamination' that is created by negative emotions and baseless beliefs. Schoenfeld (1987) and the Campione team (Campione, Brown & Connell, 1988) are of the opinion that the fact that students use few metacognitive processes when doing mathematics is attributable to the belief that mathematical problems are solved by using a series of steps which have little to do with their reality or with real problem solving.

Whether taking the form of discussion or systematic research, the current work on certain aspects of learning in relation to metacognition and certain components of the emotional dimension focus specifically on the role of intervening factors in metacognition which affect emotional responses to learning (Carr, 1996; Fasko & Skidmore, 1999; McInerney, McInerney & March, 1997). Discussion of math anxiety began in earnest in the 1970's (Tobias, 1978). Desensitization workshops in mathematics were suggested as a way to intervene directly at the emotional level. Attention was focused primarily on adults, particularly women. Little systematic research has been done on the effect of such interventions. What the studies have yielded are possible discussion points which suggest the positive effects of this type of activity. (Kogelman & Warren, 1978; Tobias, 1978, 1987).

In an attempt to provide teachers with the means to intervene in the area of emotional response and metacognition in mathematics, we undertook research (Lafortune & St-Pierre, 1994a-b, 1996) to create, develop and validate technical teaching material geared towards intervention on both fronts. An assessment of the existing material led us to the conclusion that various activities (12 categories[2]) are capable of a positive influence on math anxiety. For example, there are activities involving group discussions during which students share their opinions about mathematics. In addition, there are modeling activities in which teachers share their personal learning experiences to demonstrate that they too can have tense moments with regard to mathematics or other subjects. There are also self-evaluation activities in which, in order to lessen the tension of waiting for results, students predict the outcome of an examination. The results show that activities geared towards work methods and solving mathematical problems are the ones that arouse the greatest interest. Even if teachers are not comfortable with group discussions and collaborative teamwork, they grasp the importance of using these teaching methods. Writing activities elicit the least amount of interest and can even be put-offs for many. Talman (1992) points out that recording thoughts in a journal facilitates student/teacher communication and an environment in which students cannot avoid exploring mathematics. To write about mathematics, in particular about emotional issues, one must be aware of the feelings (including anxiety) which this subject arouses. This is the first step towards verbalization and the sharing of solutions which can in turn facilitate awareness of mental processes.

Our research has brought to light certain concepts about the teaching and learning of mathematics. It seems that the time required for certain classroom activities is a rather important constraint. Teachers wonder whether it is worth it to cut down on mathematical content in order to focus directly on emotional and metacognitive issues. They are uncomfortable with the idea of attempting experiments whose outcome they cannot control and fearful of the students' reactions. Some are even afraid of having to confront their colleagues and even themselves in defense of these new approaches. They are afraid of being forced to question their own image, evaluation methods and practices. (Lafortune & St-Pierre, 1994a-b, 1996). These observations can be examined in the light of those made by Martinez and Martinez (1996) in which they explain how traditional teaching of mathematics can increase the anxiety level of some students (writing a flawless series of steps on the board, asking students questions in front of the class and giving the impression that there is only one correct answer).

Despite the lack of research on the influence of anxiety on the development of metacognitive skills in mathematics, we assume that anxiety can exert an influence over metacognition in the ways outlined below.

Metacognitive knowledge is a student's perception of himself and his ability to solve problems. This knowledge is not always accurate but students internalize it as representing reality. One may conclude that, although they do not necessarily fail, students who are anxious about mathematics have trouble recognizing the full extent of their own abilities. They may be inclined to begin working on a mathematical problem while having difficulty understanding its terms because they are overwhelmed by the negative thoughts associated with earlier experiences or by beliefs founded on the opinions of peers (cognitive component). They may allow the tension to mount without attempting to evaluate what is taking place (emotional component).

Anxiety can also affect the management of mental activity because students who are experiencing math anxiety will try at all costs to find an answer so as to rid themselves of the discomfort brought on by the subject. Because their control and regulation process are affected by anxiety, they are often content with far-fetched answers. They may also memorize techniques or reproduce procedures introduced by the teacher.

Anxiety can also interfere with awareness of mental processes. Even if they are aware, a certain form of 'mental contamination' may cause the learners to underestimate their chosen strategy or themselves. This does not necessarily affect performance.

These assumptions about the effect of anxiety on the development of metacognitive skills have led us to advance the theory that a certain level or form of anxiety may assist or may even be necessary for the management of mental process in mathematics. It appears that the cognitive component of anxiety may help to bring disturbances in the problem solving process to the conscious mind. This awareness can help the learner to identify the source of his difficulties and take steps to lessen their effect. It is our opinion that some level of anxiety is preferable to its total absence. This then suggests indifference is demonstrated in the differences between boys and girls (Lafortune, Mongeau, Daniel & Pallascio, 2002a-b). That type of anxiety can be compared to a flickering candle flame. To keep it strong and steady, disturbing factors must be controlled. When the disturbing factors are controlled there is no anxiety, there is indifference, and there is no flame. We believe it is much harder to light a flame and keep it burning steadily thereby creating harmony.

6. Conclusions

The foregoing discussion of the effect of anxiety on the development of metacognitive skills in mathematics would seem to suggest that the emotional state brought on by anxiety can have only a negative effect on the learning of mathematics and its associated mental processes. A more systematic examination of the existing research on various aspects of the link between metacognition and emotional response reveals that very little work has been done on anxiety and metacognition in mathematics. It has also not been clearly established that the influence of anxiety on the learning of mathematics is always negative. Having examined the existing body of work we propose certain directions for future research in this area.

It is important that the effect of anxiety on metacognition in mathematics be explored and that the analysis not be confined to the negative aspects of this area of emotion. It is our belief that certain students who have a negative perception of their anxious feelings or of their own inner fears could benefit from those emotions by transforming them into excitement about solving mathematical problems. It seems to us that it would be easier to help those students – especially girls - to understand their math anxiety and to transform that emotion into a positive reaction, than it would be to awaken interest in solving mathematical problems where there is indifference – especially among boys.

Carr (1996) points out that as students' progress through their academic career the link between emotional response and grades becomes closer. It would be interesting to study that evolution of emotional response in students between 6 and 17 (pre-university) (see for example, Pons, Harris & de Rosnay, 2004). The results of the meta-analysis conducted by Ma and Kishor (1997) could be useful to such research. Research of this type could also be informed by our own research in which we asked students to 'draw mathematics' (Lafortune, 1994; Lafortune, Daniel, Pallascio & Schleifer 1999; Lafortune & Mongeau, 2003; Lafortune, Mongeau & Pallascio 2000; Lafortune, Mongeau, Daniel & Pallascio,

2002a-b). The results were surprising. At the beginning of their primary school studies the pupils' attitude towards mathematics does not seem too negative (though a bit stereotypical). At this stage they produce drawings of computers, calculators, cash registers, their teachers or a family member. Between the end of primary and the beginning of secondary studies their portrayal of mathematics is generally quite negative. The drawings which we have already analyzed (about a few hundred) depict an angel – demon duality representing the positive and negative sides of the subject. Some children depict themselves being hit on the head with a hammer, others show their own heads bursting, while others portrayed mathematics as their teacher in the form of a horned, fork-tailed devil. Some children drew themselves crying over a math script with a failing grade. Others saw themselves working at mathematics while thick black clouds hovered over their heads and flashes of lightning cut through to the brain. The drawings are even more dramatic at the end of secondary studies. Youngsters who are doing well in mathematics and those who are failing both illustrate it using images such as a child on all fours in a classroom being whipped by the teacher. Others drew a cemetery with a hand sticking out of a mound of earth and the words 'Mathematics: the deeper you dig, the deeper you get.' For some students the subject was depicted by images of war with cannons in the form of numbers. The explanatory words here were 'in math as in war, you may lose but you can never win'.

Research needs to be done on people who avoid mathematics because of the tension it arouses. This research should be directed at finding solutions for those persons who make career changes in response to the number of mathematics courses to be taken. People who do well in mathematics could be interviewed as well as others who have difficulty with it. The work done by Tobias (1990) on reasons for abandoning the sciences for other subjects would also be useful. By understanding the role of mathematics in certain persons' life stories one could better understand the choices made and reflect more meaningfully on the following questions: Does emotional response have a negative effect on cognitive and metacognitive processes? Do gaps in metacognitive skills give rise to negative emotional reactions? What is the role of math anxiety in career choice? By interviewing adults, one could exploit their self-awareness to better understand the phenomenon and find solutions which could be tested on primary school children. Carr (1996) focuses on parents' influence on mathematics learning in children. She refers to the findings of Crystal and Stevenson (1991), Stevenson, Lee, Chen, Stigler, Hsu and Kitamura (1990) and Uttal Lummie and Stevenson (1998) reporting, from a cultural perspective, on the attitudes of parents who pass on to their children their views of the importance of mathematics and of grades (see also Lafortune, 2003). Willig, Harnisch, Hill and Maehr (1983) emphasize the influence of culture on beliefs about attributes and anxiety regarding achievement in mathematics. We have begun research aimed at designing and testing a program of assistance in education involving home/school cooperation to ensure consistent attention to mathematics. Parents, teachers and children are brought together in interview groups. We have noticed a gap between what children want and what their parents are offering them. For example, we asked children whether they experienced stress when doing examinations in mathematics. Several confirmed feeling tension in such situations. They do not discuss this with their parents but would like to be able to. Parents on the other hand usually insist that their children feel no such stress. This research will allow us to develop ways of sensitizing parents so they can be more aware of their children's emotional responses. Further research could examine the effect of such an educational assistance program.

The research which we are completing on *Philosophy for Children* adapted to mathematics (SSHRC 1997 – 2000) (Lafortune, Mongeau, Daniel & Pallascio, 2000, 2002a-b; Lafortune, Mongeau & Pallascio 2000) has mixed results. Using this approach students develop significantly higher levels of belief in their ability to exercise control. They see themselves as having greater control over their own learning than do students in control groups. We have noticed, however, that this approach does not reduce math anxiety; in fact it significantly increased anxiety levels among girls. It is true this approach does not touch directly upon metacognition. However, be described as a reflexive approach which causes one to reflect upon ideas about mathematics and the learning of it rather than on one's learning process as is the case with the metacognitive approach.

This result can be compared to those of McInerney, McInerney and Marsh (1997) which showed that a non-traditional (metacognitive and cooperative) approach increased anxiety in the most anxious members of the group. Increased anxiety, when faced with an innovative approach, may be viewed as positive because it may indicate a shattering of beliefs and prejudices about mathematics. It can be disturbing to realize that the things one believed about mathematics are not exactly true; however, this is one step towards a better understanding of what 'real' mathematics can be.

Martinez and Martinez (1996) support this view by proposing ways of detecting anxiety among persons teaching mathematics. According to the authors, one must recognize and face up to one's fears and discover the particular type of problems which anxiety creates. They favor a metacognitive approach aimed at analyzing ones own thought processes relating to mathematics. This approach allows for immersion in mathematics and better comprehension of the learning processes involved. The authors also outline the behaviors and attitudes that create anxiety among students. When the teacher faces the board and speaks in a monotone while explaining a technique, students often wonder "How did the teacher do that?" or "What does that mean?". Anxiety mounts when the teacher questions a student or requests a student to go to the board to explain the problem-solving procedure. Anxiety is also very present whenever one adopts a negative attitude towards questions asked of students and the responses they give. It is not always necessary to verbalize one's judgment. Silence or any gesture of disappointment can also have just as harmful an effect. The authors add that the objective is not to rid the system of teachers who experience anxiety about mathematics. (Questionnaire responses indicate 60% are very anxious about mathematics and 30% are moderately anxious.) The aim should be to avoid behaviors and attitudes which foster anxiety in students. This realization is in keeping with the results of the meta-analysis carried out by Ma and Kishor (1997) which shows that the more students advance in their school career the more their attitude towards mathematics deteriorates and becomes negative. Some of the behavior and attitudes of teachers, expressed in various ways in class, could explain the development of these negative attitudes.

Within the framework of the metacognitive-constructivist approach to mathematics that we are proposing, we particularly suggest the use of self-evaluation to enhance the development of metacognitive skills. If we wish these self-evaluation processes to be taken into account, then educators must devote time to them and must they give feedback or get feedback from the learners on how they carry out their self-evaluation (Lafortune, 1998). Although educators are aware of the relevance of self-evaluation to the study of mathematics, this approach is not yet been used consistently.

References

Anthony, G. (1996). Active learning in a constructivist framework. *Educational Studies in Mathematics, 31*, 349-369.

Baruk, S. (1973). *Échec et maths*. Paris: Éditions du Seuil.

Baruk, S. (1977). *Fabrice ou l'école des mathématiques*. Paris: Éditions du Seuil.

Baruk, S. (1985). *L'âge du capitaine: de l'erreur en mathématiques*. Paris: Éditions du Seuil.

Baruk, S. (1989). Pourquoi des differences? In L. Lafortune (Ed.), *Quelles différences? Les femmes et l'enseignement des mathématiques* (pp. 19-50). Montréal: Remue-ménage.

Brown, A. (1987). Metacognition, executive control, self-regulation and other more mysterious mechanisms. In F. Weinert & R. Kluwe (Eds.), *Metacognition, motivation and understanding mechanisms* (pp. 515-529). New-York: Wiley.

Campione, J.C., Brown, A.L., & Connell M.L. (1988). Metacognition: On the importance of understanding what you are doing. In R.I. Charles & E.A. Silver (Eds.), *The teaching and assessing of mathematical problem solving* (pp. 93-114). Reston, VA: National Council of Teachers of Mathematics.

Carr, M. (1996). Metacognitive, motivational, and social influences on mathematics strategy use. In M. Carr (Ed.), *Motivation in mathematics* (pp. 89-111). Cresskill, NJ: Hampton Press.

Dehaene, S. (1997). *La bosse des maths*. Paris: Odile Jacob.

De Serres, M., & Groleau, J.-D. (1997). *Mathématiques et langages*. Montréal: Collège Jean-de-Brébeuf.

Doudin, P.-A., & Martin, D. (1992). *De l'intérêt de l'approche métacognitive en pédagogie*. Lausanne: CVRP.

Fasko, D., & Skidmore, R. (1999). *The effects of questions and anxiety on attention, question confidence and metacognition*. Paper, Annual Meeting of Association for the Research in Education, Québec, Canada.

Fennema, E., & Sherman, J.A. (1976). Fennema-Sherman Mathematics Attitude Scales: Instruments designed to measure attitudes toward the learning of mathematics by females and males. *JSAS Catalog of Selected Documents in Psychology, 1225*(6), 31.

Flavell, J.H. (1979). Metacognition and cognitive monitoring: A new area of cognitive developmental inquiry. *American Psychologist, 34*, 906-911.

Flavell, J.H. (1987). Speculations about the nature and development of metacognition. In F. Weinert & R. Kluwe (Eds.), *Metacognition, motivation and understanding* (pp. 21-30). Hillsdale, NJ: Lawrence Erlbaum Associates.

Goos, M., & Galbraith, P. (1996). Do it this way! Metacognitive strategies in collaborative mathematical problem solving, *Educational Studies in Mathematics, 30,* 229-260.

Hatchuel, F. (2000). *Apprendre à aimer les mathématiques.* Paris: Presses Universitaires de France.

Jitendra, A., & Xin, Y.P. (1997). Mathematical word-problem-solving instruction for students with mild disabilities and students at risk for math failure: A research synthesis, *Journal of Special Education, 30,* 412-438.

Kogelman, S., & Warren, J. (1978). Mind Over Math. New York: McGraw-Hill.

Lafortune, L. (1987). *Les Mathématiques d'appoint et les adultes : description de la situation et éléments de solution.* Québec: Ministère de l'enseignement supérieur et de la science, DGEC, SFA.

Lafortune, L. (1988). *L'Enseignement des mathématiques d'appoint aux adultes: étude des méthodes pédagogiques et des attitudes des enseignants et enseignantes.* Montréal: Cégep André-Laurendeau.

Lafortune, L. (1990). *Adultes, attitudes et apprentissages des mathématiques.* Montréal: Cégep André-Laurendeau.

Lafortune, L. (1992a). *Élaboration, implantation et évaluation d'implantation à l'ordre collégial d'un plan d'intervention andragogique en mathématiques portant sur la dimension affective en mathématiques.* Doctoral thesis, University of Québec at Montréal, Montréal, Canada.

Lafortune, L. (1992b). *Dimension affective en mathématique.* Recherche-action et matériel didactique. Mont-Royal: Modulo Éditeur.

Lafortune, L. (1994). *Des maths au-delà des mythes.* Montréal: CECM.

Lafortune, L. (1995). Diversifier pour mieux intégrer. *Instantané mathématiques,* XXXI(3), 5-15.

Lafortune, L. (1998). Une approche métacognitive-constructiviste en mathématiques. In L. Lafortune, P. Mongeau & R. Pallascio (Eds.), *Métacognition et compétences réflexives* (pp. 13-31). Montréal: Les Éditions Logiques.

Lafortune, L. (2003). Le suivi parental en mathématiques. Intervenir sur les croyances. In L. Lafortune, C. Deaudelin, P.-A. Doudin & D. Martin (Eds.), *Conceptions, croyances et représentations en maths, sciences et technos* (pp. 121-145). Québec: Presses de l'Université du Québec.

Lafortune, L, Daniel, M.F., Pallascio, R., & Schleifer, M. (1999). Evolution of pupils' attitudes to mathematics when using a philosophical approach. *Analytic Teaching, 20*(1), 33-44.

Lafortune, L. & Mongeau, P. (2003). Approche des mathématiques par le dessin: une analyse qualitative et quantitative de dessins. In L. Lafortune, C. Deaudelin, P.-A. Doudin & D. Martin (Eds.), *Conceptions, croyances et représentations en maths, sciences et technos* (pp. 91-100). Québec: Presses de l'Université du Québec.

Lafortune, L., Mongeau, P., & Pallascio, R. (2000). Une mesure des croyances et préjugés à l'égard des mathématiques. In R. Pallascio & L. Lafortune (Eds.), *Pour une pensée réflexive en education* (pp. 209-232). Québec: Presses de l'Université du Québec.

Lafortune, L., Mongeau, P., Daniel, M.-F., & Pallascio, R. (2000). Approche philosophique des mathématiques et affectivité: premières measures. In R. Pallascio & L. Lafortune (Eds.), *Pensée réflexive en éducation* (pp. 181-208). Saint-Foy: Presses de l'Université du Québec.

Lafortune, L., Mongeau, P., Daniel, M.-F., & Pallascio, R. (2002a). Anxiété à l'égard des mathématiques: applications et mise à l'essai d'une approche philosophique. In L. Lafortune & P. Mongeau (Eds.), *L'affectivité dans l'apprentissage* (pp. 49-79). Sainte-Foy: Presses de l'Université du Québec.

Lafortune, L., Mongeau, P., Daniel, M.-F., & Pallascio, R. (2002b). Philosopher sur les mathématiques: Évolution du concept de soi et des croyances attributionnelles de contrôle. In L. Lafortune & P. Mongeau (Eds.), *L'affectivité dans l'apprentissage* (pp. 27-48). Sainte-Foy: Presses de l'Université du Québec.

Lafortune, L., & St-Pierre, L. (1994a). *La pensée et les émotions en mathématiques. Métacognition et affectivité*. Montréal: Les Éditions Logiques.

Lafortune, L., & St-Pierre, L. (1994b). *Les processus mentaux et les émotions dans l'apprentissage*. Montréal: Les Éditions Logiques.

Lafortune, L., & St-Pierre, L. (1996). *L'affectivité et la métacognition dans la classe*. Montréal: Les Éditions Logiques.

Lucangeli, D., & Cornoldi, C. (1999). Métacognition et mathématiques. In P.-A. Doudin, D. Martin & O. Albanese (Eds.), *Métacognition et education* (pp. 265-294). Berne, Peter Lang.

Ma, X., & Kishor, N. (1997). Assessing the relationship between attitude toward mathematics and achievement in mathematics: A meta-analysis. *Journal for Research in Mathematics Education, 28*(1), 26-47.

Martin, D., Doudin, P.-A,. & Albanese, O. (2001). Vers une psychopégagogie metacognitive. In P.-A. Doudin, D. Martin & O. Albanese (Eds.), *Métacognition et éducation. Aspects transversaux et disciplinaires* (pp. 3-30). Berne: Peter Lang.

Martinez, J.G.R., & Martinez, N.C. (1996). *Math without fear*. Boston: Allyn and Bacon.

McInerney, V., McInerney, D.M., & Marsh, H.W. (1997). Effects of metacognitive strategy training within a cooperative group learning context on computer achievement and anxiety: An aptitude-treatment interaction study. *Journal of Educational Psychology, 89*(4), 686-695.

McLoed, D.B. (1994). Research on affect and mathematics learning in the JRME 1970 to the present. Journal for Research in Mathematics Education, 25(6), 637-647.

Meece, J.L., Wigfield, A., & Eccles, J.S. (1990). Predictors of math anxiety and its influence on young adolescents' course enrollment intentions and performance in mathematics, *Journal of Educational Psychology, 82*(1), 60-70.

Meravech, Z.R., & Kramarski, B. (1997). A multidimensional method for teaching mathematics in heterogeneous classrooms. *American Educational Research Journal, 34*, 365-394.

Ministère de l'éducation (2001). *Troisième enquête internationale sur la mathématique et les sciences – TEIMS-99: Rapport du Québec*. Québec: Gouvernement du Québec.

Naveh-Benjamin, M., McKeachie, W.J., & Lin, Y.G. (1987). Two types of test-anxious students : Support for an information-processing model. *Journal of Educational Psychology, 79*, 131-136.

Nimier, J. (1976). *Mathématiques et affectivité*. Paris: Stock.

Nimier, J. (1985). *Les maths, le français, les langues, à quoi ça me sert?* Paris: Nathan.

Petit, M., & Zawojwoski, J.S. (1997). Teachers and students learning together about assessing problem solving. *Mathematics Teacher, 90*, 472-477.

Pons, F., Doudin, P.-A., Martin, D., Lafortune, L., & Harris, P.L. (2004). Psychogenèse de la conscience et pensée réflexive. In R. Pallascio, M.-F. Daniel & L. Lafortune (Eds.), *Pensée et réflexivité: théories et pratiques éducatives* (pp. 13-36). Sainte-Foy: Presses de l'Université du Québec.

Pons, F., & Harris, P.L. (2001). Piaget's conception of the development of consciousness: An examination of two hypotheses. *Human Development, 44*(4), 220-227.

Pons, F., Harris, P.L., & de Rosnay, M. (2004). Emotion comprehension between 3 and 11 years: Developmental periods and hierarchical organizations. *European Journal of Developmental Psychology, 1*(2), 127-152.

Schoenfeld, A.H. (1987). What's all the fuss about metacognition? In A.H. Schoenfeld (Ed.), *Cognitive science and mathematics education* (pp. 189-215). Hillsdale, NJ: Lawrence Erlbaum.

St-Hilaire, F. (1989). De l'influence des mathématiques sur le foie. In L Lafortune (Ed.), *Quelles différences? Les femmes et l'enseignement des mathématiques* (pp. 115-120). Montréal: Remue-Ménage.

Talman, L.A. (1992). Weekly journal entries – an effective tool for teaching mathematics. In A. Sterrett (Ed.), *Using writing to teach mathematics* (pp. 107-110). Washington, DC: MAA.

Tobias, S. (1978). *Over-coming math anxiety*. Boston, MA: Houghton Mifflin.

Tobias, S. (1987). *Succeed with math: Every student's guide to conquering math anxiety*. New-York, NY: College Entrance Examination Board.

Tobias, S. (1990). *They're not dumb, they're different: Stalking the second tier*, Tucson, AZ: Research Corporation, A foundation for the advancement of science.

Tousignant, J. (1999), *Séminaire de réflexion portant sur la situation de la mathématique, de la science et de la technologie au Québec*, Québec: Gouvernement du Québec.

Viau, R. (1995). L'état des recherches sur l'anxiété en contexte scolaire. *Cahiers de la recherche en éducation, 2*(2), 375-398.

Weyl-Kailey, L. (1985). *Victoire sur les maths*. Paris: Robert Laffont.

Wigfield, A., & Eccles, J.S. (1989). Test anxiety in elementary and secondary school students, *Educational Psychologist, 24*, 159-183.

Wilson, T.D., Gilbert, D.T., & Wheatley, T.P. (1998). Protecting our minds: The role of lay beliefs. In V.Y Yzerbyt, G. Lories & B. Dardenne (Ed.), *Metacognition: Cognitive and social dimensions* (pp. 171-201). London: Sage Publications.

Zaslavsky, C. (1994). Fear of math: *How to get over it and get on with your life*. New Brunswick, NJ: Rutgers University Press.

---

[1] Research funded by the Social Sciences and Humanities Research Council of Canada (Lafortune, Daniel, Pallascio, Mongeau et Schleifer, SSHRC, 1997-2000).

[2] These 12 categories refer to the collaborative team work, group discussion, play acting and simulations, producing schematas, modelling activities, feedback, evaluation, self-evaluation, observation and self-observation, writing activities or reading.

CHAPTER 8

A view of emotions and learning

Mogens Jensen

1. Introduction

This chapter analyzes some aspects of emotions, and the role they play as we perceive various situations. This is accomplished through a selection of aspects oriented towards learning processes. The theoretical considerations are illustrated by analyzing three examples of learning processes from the empirical work of others. The result is a focus on emotional aspects of learning-situations and the impact of this emotional experience on the learning processes. This leads to reflections on teaching and the task of the teacher in terms of developing heuristics for analyzing and intervening in learning processes, rather than giving precise directions for teaching.

"Emotion" is a concept used in many contexts both within and outside psychology. It is also part of folk-psychology (Bruner, 1990). Folk-psychology is part of the explanation of the state of the concept. It has a rather fuzzy meaning. For our purpose, we will talk about two aspects of the way humans experience their everyday life – emotion and feeling.

Emotion refers to an evaluation of a situation in its totality. It is a state we experience in relation to a situation. This state is experienced with bodily aspects, a mood and a tendency to act. It involves an evaluation of the importance of the situation for the person and an evaluation of the problems and possibilities in relation to personal goals (Albertsen, 2003; Oatley & Jenkins, 1996). Emotions are not as stable as feelings across time; however, there is a tendency to evaluate comparable situations in the same way. Emotions are developed in cultural settings and are inherited. Inherited or natural emotions (Ekman & Friesen, 1971) span across cultures in addition to those that originate in the specific culture (Harre, 1986).

Feelings refer to an aspect of our relation to other people and objects. They evaluate the value we assign our relation to these people and objects. Feelings operate in the dimensions of positive – negative, important and central – more marginal, soothing – instrumental, etc. They are relatively stable across time. When changes appear, they are usually gradual.

2. Emotions in psychology

The discussion of the relation between emotion and cognition has a long history in psychology (Zajonc, 1980; Oatley & Jenkins, 1996). Several experiments have been designed and carried out to determine whether cognition or emotion comes first in the apprehension of the situation. This discussion depends on the distinction between emotion and cognition. For our purpose, the distinction between emotion and cognition need not be sharp. As we discuss emotions and feelings, it is important to stress that problems in learning can be caused by purely cognitive processes; however, that is not the focus of this chapter. Included in our discussions of an emotional experience, is an evaluation of the situation in its totality. It will be summed up and put in relation to our prior experience of total situations and our present goals (Oatley & Jenkins, 1996; Albertsen, 2003). It even includes a tendency to act in order to handle the situation, although the action is still not precise in its direction.

Human functions have been developed differently throughout the history of evolution. Examining history allows us to understand the task the function was developed to solve (Cosmides & Tooby, 1995; Reber, 1992). In the evolution of the brain there are structures we have in common with other mammals. This is called the early mammal brain (McLean, 1985). This part of our brain is dominated by the limbic system, and is the place where emotional functions are anchored on a physical level. When we were living as hunter-gatherers, we needed an ability to evaluate a given situation quickly and act quickly. We had to fly or be ready to fight. This function is described as emotional experience.

Later in evolution our neo-cortex developed further than other mammals. The neo-cortex is mainly involved in more complex analysis of our perceptions and in planning, but there is a complex interplay between neo-cortex and the limbic system. The neo-cortex contains many centers that inhibit actions, whereas the limbic system and other lower parts of the brain contain many centers that facilitate actions (Borchgrevink, 1997). These connected systems constitute the neurological foundation that regulates the necessary behavior, such as acting quickly to survive, yet postponing action in order to analyze and plan.

In the ontological development of our brain the limbic system matures before the neo-cortex (Smith, 1996; Johnson, 1997). This correlates with the experience that toddlers cannot always inhibit actions that fulfill needs, such as taking a candy; however, adults are generally able to do so. It also illustrates the natural priorities of development, such as, survival comes first and reflection or more detailed analysis and understanding of experience comes second.

Emotion is an evaluation of the situation in its totality; therefore, the evaluation might include unimportant factors which are endowed with importance. Because of our prior experiences, the evaluation of a given situation may be re-adjusted when we experience similar situations. Neisser (1976) provides a description of the development of concepts in which he draws a hermeneutic circle. The concept gives you an understanding with which you perceive the situation. However, the perception is at the same time evaluated in order to adjust the concept with the present experience. The same description can be used on the dynamic of developing emotional experience. This also implies, that children do not have the abilities to evaluate situations as precisely as adults; therefore, they will make more wrong conclusions about which factors are of importance and which are unessential. A crucial point in the development of emotions is this differentiation. A cognitive-behavioral explanation of phobias follows these lines: situations have been evaluated incorrectly; thus giving importance to an irrelevant aspect of the situation. For example, a dreadful experience in which a rabbit was present is connected to the fur of the rabbit giving a phobia of furs. Even if we don't go as far as phobias we might focus on wrong aspects of certain situations and then our emotions will depend on "unessential factors". One example is a phenomenon called "qualitative illiteracy". Qualitative illiteracy represents people who learned to read in school, but this experience was filled with anxiety; consequently, they do not read after leaving school unless they are forced to. In some years their ability to read will diminish. This description of the emotional evaluation of learning situations is captured by the concept of co-learning. While you learn something, you develop a judgment of value, pleasure, etc. in relation to the context of learning. As illustrated by qualitative illiteracy, this co-learning can have great impact on ones willingness to spend time with the topic later on. A consequence of this dynamic in development is that children are more inclined to make these connections than adults.

Co-learning connects to the old psychological question of making a distinction between figure and background prototypically illustrated with the figure of a vase or of two faces presented by Rubin. Perceiving a complex situation implies sorting out which elements are of importance and which are backgrounds without importance. One of the problems in infantile autism seems to be problems creating gestalts in the perception of situations (Frith & Happé, 1995). Many behavioral problems in relation to autism originate in children with autism giving importance to elements which we see as unimportant as in the way chairs are standing in the dining room: autistic children can't calm down when chairs are standing in an unusual way. They see the order of the chairs as an important part of the figure, where as we see it as an unimportant part of the background. Much of this evaluation is processed outside of consciousness. This is reasonable because the capacity of consciousness is rather slow and has limited capacity (Miller, 1956). Still it can give some backlash because you might make a wrong evaluation. Normally later experiences will correct you, but this is not always the case. Repeated experience will strengthen the correctness of your evaluation. However, selective perception can give you misleading feedback and you might withhold a wrong evaluation. This will give you an irregular emotional experience that is founded more on your own experience than on the present situation. Experiences loaded with much intensity will often be retained stronger than more common daily experiences, especially if they are evaluated negatively. This again can be explained in an evolutionary model because negative situations are more important to remember and learn from in order to survive than are positive ones.

As emotional evaluation of situations is processed outside consciousness, participants are not aware of which clues contribute to the evaluation. In order to understand an emotional evaluation – or to evaluate the evaluation you might say – you have to do this in relation to the specific situation or context (Fog, 1985). To understand the reaction of a pupil in a situation concerning learning, we will have to discuss specific situations and not general patterns. Discussing specific situations gives us the opportunity to discover which clues are used in the emotionally evaluation of the situation. Later we can conclude general patterns across the specific situations that were considered.

Another aspect of the unconscious processing of emotional evaluation is considerations concerning conscious developing of ones own emotional evaluation. You can get such clear reactions from the environment on your evaluations, that you can develop them on this basis. However, if you are to take responsibility for your own learning process, the learning process must involve reflections on your evaluations. By reflecting on your own experience you enhance observations and put them into verbal language, which is more convenient for analyzing the experience. These situations are complex and partly evaluated outside consciousness, so it is important to analyze concrete, specific situations. Although you have not used all of the information in your interpretation of the situation, you still have some perception of this un-used information and it can be used in such an analysis. Discussing concrete situations enables you to incorporate aspects that do not fit with your former evaluation and allows you to change and develop your emotional evaluations. The function of the cortex, especially the frontal lobes, is used for changing your way of experiencing, providing the inhibiting effect of the frontal lobes can postpone action until further analysis has come about.

3. Development of feelings

The newborn child is almost helpless, but he has two ways of handling this situation. He can relate actively to others, and he can learn everything necessary in due time. An important aspect of relating to significant others (Mead, 1934) is the aim of establishing security, and as surviving is more important than qualifying for future challenges in a given situation, security has priority over learning. Since the infant has little experience, he will accept the evaluation of situations given to him by these significant others. The emotional evaluation of a situation is therefore closely connected to feelings, as both influence the development of the other.

Bowlby (1969, 1988) has formulated a theory of attachment, which describes some of the dynamics of relating between child and mother. The child has a biologically founded repertoire of behaviors that call for the mother to care for the child. These are called "attachment behaviors" (Bowlby, 1969). There is a theoretical discussion concerning when attachment behaviors show up in the development of the child and which actions can be called attachment behavior. In general, the child is seen as an active participant in establishing relations to adults very early on. Some even interpret behavior right from birth as attachment behavior. An important concept in attachment-theory is the secure base (Bowlby, 1988). The mother is used as a secure base from which the child seeks out in the world to explore it and learn. The prototypical situation is in the waiting room of the doctor's office. In this situation, the child stays close to his mother in the beginning. Then he moves out in the room looking at the toys. Time and again he comes back to mother to reestablish security. As he gets older, looking at the mother will suffice. When new situations occur that might be dangerous (i.e. the entrance of a new patient into the waiting room) the tendency to connect to the secure base increases.

Three aspects of this description are worth noting. When the child evaluates the situation as potentially dangerous, he contacts the secure base i.e. mother for an evaluation of the situation. This means that the evaluation of the situation (what we earlier on have called "emotional experience") is partly learned from those who constitute the secure base in the life of the child. Of course some situations are so chaotic and threatening that no learning is possible. In this little act of learning about the world many cultural standards of social acting are exercised. The literature on attachment-theory is filled with examples of children achieving different attitudes towards other people (Colin, 1996). Another aspect is the priority of security before learning. We touched upon this aspect earlier from a neuropsychological angle. When the child feels insecure, his behavior will concentrate on re-establishing security by connecting with the secure base. The exploration of the world or the learning process is postponed. In a given situation this could lead to consideration of the psychodynamic balance of the child. In a situation where the child feels safe, the balance is very positive and gives a surplus for learning new things. In a situation where the child is feeling rather insecure, the focus will be on security and the surplus for learning will be smaller if there is any at all. The third aspect is the importance of obtaining a relation to adults. Stern (1995) has a number of examples from clinical work on children submitting to the expectationsn that they perceive their mothers have. Security is more important and the wishes of the child give way (Stern, 1995). Bruner (1990) talks about the constituting process of the individual. Every human is born with some biologically founded potential. The personality is constituted in the interplay between this biology and the context in which they grow up. More specific this goes for the view of oneself and ones own emotions too. This point is very much in line with constructionist theories of today (Fischer et al., 1997). To put this third aspect in another way you could say, that humans are more likely to learn from people they have close relations to. Especially when learning about topics which connect closely to their way of experiencing the world and to their own personality. When considering the development of a child in a new environment, it is important to determine which people to rely on. Relying on people who engage in your security or people who are interested in the way you experience the situation seems to be a fairly good strategy. When a person experiences somebody who is authentically interested in his interests, wishes and way of experiencing the specific situation, this will enhance his openness for learning from this person (Løvlie Schibbye 2002; Bae, 1996). This aspect can be conceptualized as an attitude of recognition from the teacher towards the learner. Used on teaching this emphasizes the importance of the feelings of the pupils towards the teacher.

This can also be explicated in terms of attachment-theory. Being together with somebody, who you perceive as interested in your way of experiencing and thinking will make you more comfortable. You will experience support and feel more secure; and thereby, have a surplus for learning.

When growing up we gradually employ other ways of staying secure. These include such things as leaning on well-known locations and leaning on one's own competence. The use of locations as a source of security begins early and increases throughout childhood. Being in familiar locations causes most people to relax. This is connected to our experience of competence because familiar locations strengthen our competence to predict what will happen and to act appropriately. The tendency to want to be able to predict a situation is supported by studies of the reaction of people in crisis. They use a lot of energy to find an explanation of the situation they experienced. They may even go to the extent of including luck, destiny, etc. (Rothbaum et al., 1982). It is very hard to live with chance as an aspect of life. This is illustrated in evolution. It is reasonable because the struggle to understand and predict is a way of enhancing your competencies to survive similar situations in the future. When these observations are connected with the previous information, it becomes apparent that it is important for learning processes and how you experience the world that you are together with persons you see as having an attitude of recognition. Your feelings for other persons influence your psychodynamic balance. The same knowledge concerning security in locations and routines is depicted in work about people with infantile autism and with severely handicapped conditions. Here a highly structured day is used as a way of increasing security, since relations are more difficult to establish because of the specific handicap in autism. The highly structured day is a precondition for learning and developing (Jordan, 1995).

4. Emotions and feelings resumed

In the analysis above emotions and feelings are separated as two concepts though connected and overlapping. The purpose has been to focus on some characteristic aspects of both.

Emotions are described as instant evaluation of a whole situation. This process is going on outside awareness which raises some constraints when we want to develop this evaluation. An important condition is the ability to inhibit the actions connected with the evaluation long enough to reflect on new aspects of the situation. This is both a question of maturity of the brain and of training. When one is not aware of the circumstances used for the evaluation, co-learning can go wrong. The activity is judged on false premises, and this judgment can influence engagement in future activity.

Feelings are influencing the development of your knowledge of the world. As an infant you rely very much on the evaluation of significant others (Mead) whom you use as your secure base. This pattern influence learning because you rely more upon those who make you feel secure. Teaching thus would be more efficient if the teacher shows an attitude of genuine recognition towards the pupil – the psychodynamic balance will be more positive. An overview of the development of the child indicates the priority of security before learning meaning that an insecure climate will diminish learning.

5. Examples

The following three examples are collected from empirical work on learning. Some of the results support and illustrates the previous theoretical analysis.

Learning disabilities (Example 1)

In a case study on learning disabilities McDermott (1993) discuses three different ways of analyzing learning disabilities illustrated with the case of Adam. Adam has been assessed as having learning disabilities, but as McDermott points out you can see this as 1) a problem resided only in Adam, 2) a problem of the match between the competencies of Adam and the demands of the context, and finally 3) learning disabilities as a culturally invented category which is used by part of the society – primarily the educational system – to legitimize their existence and their status on competence and knowledge and thereby needing to categorize some children as having learning disabilities. The case of Adam is discussed very much in terms of cognitive and social problems, but I will use it in discussing the influence of emotional aspects on learning processes.

Adam is 8-9 years old and is observed in test- and classroom-situations, in a cooking club, and in his spare time. He is always interested and eager to do what is expected of him; however, his success is seen as inconsistent in various contexts. In his spare time he appears to be quite normal. In the cooking club he does well when he cooperates with his friend Peter, but when he has to work with others or on his own, he fails. In the classroom he uses different acts for escaping situations in which he will be examined. He participates actively when all the pupils are engaged in instructions and collaborative activities. In test-situations he does poorly. He gives extreme guesses without trying to think or perhaps even without hearing all the questions. Some of his classmates are eager to point out his failures.

Analyzed from the angle of match between Adam and the demands of the context, the situations are graded on difficulty of the competencies starting from spare time via cooking club to classroom-situations and finally with testing as the most difficult. This is based upon the differences in the support the context provides for acting appropriate, where the support is seen as greatest in spare time and the test situation in principle gives no support at all. This hierarchy of the situations could be questioned: if you look at the demands from an aspect of emotional judgment, the spare time might as well demand more complex skills in judging importance of the factors in the situation, the impact of the situation and in negotiating your participation and achieving a positive outcome. Though he has problems in school, Adam might have developed advanced skills in some aspects (Fischer et al.). The important point here is that Adam will experience the situation as a whole, so it doesn't make sense for the teacher to look only at the cognitive demands. Situations similar in cognitive demands can be quite diverse in emotional demands and vice versa, and because the emotional pressure is affecting the cognitive functions, a teacher has to be aware of both.

Adam does well in spare time situations; therefore, he can relax and feel secure. However, in testing situations he does poorly. This makes him uncomfortable and his need for security will rise. His need for security may even rise to the degree where more rational cognitive activity is postponed until security is assured as mentioned in the theoretical analyses. This will not happen in the testing situation because no acts of creating security are allowed. The tradition of testing is based on a principle of giving equal conditions for each pupil; however, such equal conditions rarely include emotional climate. Therefore, if only cognitive conditions are examined, then Adam will not receive equal opportunities.

If we examine the situation in the classroom, Adam apparently feels comfortable and secure when he is part of the group. This is illustrated when they gather for instruction or demonstration. However, he seems to feel uncomfortable when there is risk of being questioned about the topics. His behavior can be described as using the group as a secure base, but when he is pulled out of the group, he feels insecure. Consequently, he invents strategies that lead attention to something else; this is classed as a behavioral problem. From his way of experiencing, there is logic behind his behavior. In his mind security is more important than learning. It will be difficult to extinguish this behavior if he does not find security in another way.

As mentioned at the beginning of the chapter the experience we have of ourselves depends on the reactions of other people, especially people who are important to us. Adam seems to be fighting to establish himself as a part of the group of classmates. This means he is not deviating much. If we are right in describing him as using the group as a secure base while in school, then this fight is even more important for him. This also makes him anxious about being seen as different. For example, he became anxious when he could not answer questions or follow the recipe when cooking. His surplus on the psychodynamic balance for learning is fragile. He must constantly be on his toes and ready to defend his identity and maneuvers to ensure his secure base. He might have "pure cognitive disabilities" too, but the conditions for developing his abilities are not good. Adam is described as being eager and positive, yet he could experience co-learning in school that creates an environment that defeats and threatens his identity. Hence, school may become a place that does not recognize his special needs and enable him to learn. Support for this interpretation is the relative success in the cooking club. When his good friend Peter is present he feels accepted and is doing remarkably better. The psychodynamic balance leaves more room for facing challenges.

In this case, interventions concentrating only on cognitive problems would probably fail. Removing Adam to a special education class might help in the beginning, because it would be a smaller and more secure context. However, transferring these results of the special education classroom to the normal class could easily fail because of the emotional-feeling side of the problem was not necessarily changed.

Teaching of physics (Example 2)

Bang (1998) analyzes the concept of skill from the perspective of ecological psychology – where perception is seen as an active collection of data necessary for an appropriate interpretation of the situation (Gibson,

1986) – and in the tradition of activity-theory within the cultural-historical tradition of Vygotsky and Leontjev. Her aim is to get closer to the learning process as she illustrates her ideas through the teaching of physics in grammar school. The example concerns the use of diagrams in a discussion of speed, acceleration and a free fall. She wants to describe an alternative to the traditional case in which learning is often described as an activity where the student has to outdistance the learning content in order to make some abstract conclusions about the laws of nature, etc. Every context is seen as filled with confusing and irrelevant details, and the learning process as consisting of extracting the important cues.

As an alternative Bang describes learning as developing a skill in reading the context, which contains both explicit and implicit information – in example in the diagram. The teacher is able to read a great deal of information from the diagram, but the student doesn't perceive this information at all. In the learning process this skill in reading the environment develops and the student too becomes able to perceive the implicit information directly. The learning process is seen as an act in which the student "sticks" his knowledge on the environment in a way where the environment at a first glance shows the information of interest – both explicit and implicit information. Learning is not an activity of outdistancing and abstraction, but one of engagement with the environment, where the learner becomes more closely related to the environment. Described in this way, learning processes result in a different relation between student and environment (Mammen, 1986) and this gives the student new degrees of freedom in his way of understanding, experimenting and acting on the environment.

This way of describing skills in science is parallel with another description made in a report from a research-group on the teaching of mathematics (Niss & Højgaard Jensen, 2002). In it, researchers point to the skill of asking questions in a mathematical way as being one of the important skills in mathematics. It is not just a way of abstracting from the concrete, but a way of experiencing and having a dialogue with the context in which you live. Comparing this description with our description of emotional evaluation of a context shows surprising similarities between some of the skills of science and emotions. The real environment is complex and it is important to be able to directly perceive the pertinent information and to react.

If we build on this parallel, the emotional evaluation does not focus on the logic or arguments of the dynamic of the situation. It focuses mainly on the result; hence the usefulness of the evaluation in terms of a development of the situation which is acceptable for the student. In the development of emotions we emphasized the importance of reflections, through which the evaluation of the situation can be improved. These reflections demand a situation in which we feel secure enough to postpone actions, and they have to use concrete situations as starting points. These concrete situations contain information that was not used in the first place. Thus, the information can be used to develop a new interpretation of the situation. An important part of this reflection and a good starting point consists of verbalizing which perceptions or information were used and how they were used. Such verbalizing constitutes an interest in and recognition of the way the learner experiences the situation – a recognizing attitude. Verbalizing perceptions and information in this manner allows the learner to discover which perceptions or information were excluded from the first evaluation.

These considerations stress the importance of a secure climate during teaching. They also illustrate the value of the information the teacher can gain from the way the learners act and think. Hundeide (1985) suggests the information lies not so much in whether they answer correctly or not, but in the way they act and think which depicts the way they perceive the world. The teacher could look upon learners as being from another culture and perceiving the world in a different way. If you teach and see the goal of the teaching as an enculturation – as a training of skills for acting in a different culture – then the interest in the "wrong" answers of the students is shifted because they are in fact a source of information on how the students perceive the situation (Hundeide, 1985). You will also focus more on the perception of the situation and the topics in curriculum rather than on the correct answers.

One starting point of teaching could be to investigate in collaboration with the students the consequences of the way they perceive a given topic. The next step would be to demonstrate the advantages of the perceptual approach used in curriculum – i.e. the forces of an understanding based on physics. This process will cause the students to feel pressure to consciously consider the topic and verbalize how they experience the topic. In relation to co-learning, this would enhance the possibilities of the students taking charge of their own learning. The attitude of the teacher changes from delivering the right explanations to demonstrating the advantages of these explanations. They explore the topic in relation to how students perceive the world. It also encourages students to use the content of science as a tool for solving problems, rather than learning a set of abstract laws. In relation to feelings we pointed to the picture that learners make of themselves on the basis of reactions from others, especially from people they know. This was also considered in example one concerning Adam, who was very much aware of the reaction of his classmates.

In our culture there are many expectations on abilities in science. For example, some propose that women have fewer abilities than men. This is in great part caused by cultural expectations, which is demonstrated in experimental psychology (McIntyre et al., 2003; Schmader, 2002). These investigations illustrate that the results each individual achieves is dependent upon his or her own expectations. Our expectations are developed continuously during life with childhood as the starting period upon which later experiences are built.

Describing the learning process as achieving competencies in perceiving the important information in our environment pinpoints the learning as an epistemological process wherein you discard the way you used to perceive the world in the benefit of another perception. No wonder this process can cause anxiety in the situation. In order to question your way of perceiving the world and start experimenting with another one, you have to experience the situation as rather secure.

Apprentices in electronics (Example 3)

As part of her Ph.D. thesis Tanggaard Pedersen (2004) followed apprentices in electronics in their changing educational progress. (In Denmark such an education consists of periods of school courses interchanging with periods of practical work in industries. The teachers at the special schools are often craftsmen who are also qualified as teachers). The study was done in the tradition of practice-learning, which is well known from Lave & Wenger (1991). The analysis of Tanggaard Pedersen (2004) highlights some aspects of the learning processes during the education of craftsmen. She illustrates some important aspects of emotions and feelings in learning processes.

When the apprentices work in industry, they are also occupied with routine-work, which does not require the qualifications they have received at school. This is especially true in the first part of their trainee periods. These periods can be seen as a chance for learning the culture of the work place and of the culture of the trade or the craftsmanship. Some apprentices drop out because they cannot hold on to their goal during these periods. Often they perceive these periods as boring and meaningless; whereas others can adapt to the cultures and gain popularity which allows them to feel supported during later work. This period could be seen as having a "hidden curriculum" concerning enculturation. It is hidden because it is not formulated in the official curriculum. The process is an example of co-learning in which attention is focused on practical work tasks while at the same time enculturation is a critical parameter. Apprentices who drop out fail on the hidden curriculum. Verbalization of the hidden curriculum would probably help some apprentices. This demands that educational organizations consider the aspects and learning processes centering these kinds of topics. Such considerations will enable them to learn a great deal from studying the development of emotional evaluations.

In the tradition of practice-learning the content of learning is illustrated as being connected with the context in which it is learned. Learning the culture of both the organization and the craftsmanship is learning a way of experiencing situations at work. The social aspects and the problems you have to deal with will be experienced in a way in which certain contingencies are implicit to participants. If you cannot experience in this way, you will have a hard time socially fitting in and solving problems. This description of the trajectories of learning (Dreier, 1999) that apprentices go through shows remarkable similarities to the description of emotional evaluation of a situation. They have to learn to perceive and experience situations in specific ways, not just concerning some aspects but in terms of evaluating the whole situation in its totality. It also parallels the description of learning science in the second example, where skills are seen more in line with ability in perceiving the implicit information of the environment rather than seeing it as abstract and context-free knowledge that has to be applied to the specific context. When these considerations are connected to the concept of culture, some possible angles for teaching become apparent.

In one of the intermediate periods, where the apprentices are attending school, the interplay between teacher and apprentices is described. The apprentices are more interested and engaged when the teacher tells stories or episodes depicting his or her own experiences. The success and authority of the teacher is partly dependent on his or her ability to connect the theoretical curriculum to real life experiences. As the apprentices in Tanggaard Pedersen (2004) learn from teachers and craftsmen, they develop several contingencies. She mentions that they establish a minimum of agreement on a horizon of the future between the teacher, craftsman and apprentices. A horizon of the future depicts your expectations of future tasks and qualifications needed at work. This is an important aspect of the relation between people. Attachment theory establishes that children tend to learn more from their parents than from other people, when learning is concerned with the way of experiencing or the (emotional) evaluation of a situation. As you move from experiencing situations with significant others to experiencing situations in the outside world, you have to judge whether people are reliable enough to learn from. If you experience people who have the same horizon of the future, you experience somebody who is interested in your future and your way of seeing the world. This is an important clue in your judgment. Earlier on we called this an attitude of recognition. Although many of these processes operate outside consciousness, apprentices often criticize their teachers for not making adequate connections to the reality of the working place. The apprentices' criticisms can be caused by a lack of recognition on the part of the teacher.

6. Conclusions

In order to describe more precisely the influence of emotions on learning processes, we have distinguished between emotions and feelings. The proposal is that if emotions are seen as evaluations of the present situation in its totality, this evaluation will influence the learning outcome – analyzed by use of the concept of co-learning. These emotional processes are for a great part going on outside awareness, but the result will influence future interest and activity in relation to the content of the learning. If learning experiences are negative, this will affect the intended content of the learning process. These considerations force us to consider the emotional climate in school. If we are interested in pupils learning competences not just for examination but for use in later life, it has to be learned in a positive atmosphere.

This atmosphere is somewhat dependent on an attitude of recognition from the teacher towards the pupils. This attitude has the extra advantage that it – at the same time – gives the teacher information on how to improve teaching. When the teacher is searching for an understanding of the way the pupils experience the situation and the topics of teaching, rather than just focusing on correcting wrong answers, he will also find out where the pupils go wrong. If we look at learning as a process of enculturation, the teacher has to be able to understand the way in which the pupils experience the topics. Then he can introduce another angle – i.e. the way of putting questions in science – and discuss the advantages of this with the pupils. This will also leave room for curiosity as a central part of the process of learning.

Seeing learning as a process of enculturation also points to the stress of learning. Very often learning will involve new ways of experiencing the world. This process of giving up old worldviews and accepting new ones can be threatening to some pupils. If a pupil is blocked very hard on a topic, the teacher should consider the situation of the pupil. For the pupil the process is part of a total experience, and it can shake his basic assumptions or his trust in the world of his parents. This psychodynamic balance of security versus openness for learning changes over time, and it is also influenced by other parts of the life of the pupil as quarrels with palls or parents. In extreme situations, each of us would prioritize security before learning. The important point is, that it is the way the pupil experiences the situation which makes the difference – not the way the teacher sees it.

In this chapter humans are seen as curious and eager to learn. Sometimes this curiosity can be blocked. In these situations reflections on the emotional aspects of the learning process are important, as pupils don't separate the learning processes from the rest of their life. We become better at making this separation during our life, but depending on the situation it will always influence our learning. For professionals it is therefore important to be aware of the dynamics of the emotional aspects of learning processes. It is important to emphasize that emotional aspects of learning processes are not only a question of blocking; they also provide a deeper understanding of the learning process itself.

References

Ainsworth, M.D. (1979). Infant – mother attachment. *American Psychologist*, 34(10) 932-937.

Albertsen, K. (2003). Motivation – mellem mening og betydning. In A. Aboulafia, H. Hybschmann Hansen, T. Hansen & J. Bang, (Eds.) *Virksomhed, betydning og mening* (pp. 199-210). Roskilde: Roskilde Universitets Forlag.

Bae, B. (1996). *Det interessante i det alminnelige*. Oslo: Pedagogisk Forum.

Bang, J. (1998). Læring og kompetence. *Psyke og Logos*, 19, 415-434.

Borchgrevink, H.M. (1997) "On brain function : Consequences for neuropsychological and neuromotor diagnostic assessment of multisensory impaired children. *Developmental Brain Dysfunction*, 10(4), 172-186.

Bowlby, J. (1969). *Attachement*. London: Pimlico.

Bowlby, J. (1988). *A secure base*. London: Routledge.

Bruner, J. (1990). *Acts of meaning*. Cambridge, MA: Harvard University Press.

Colin, V.L. (1996). *Human attachment*. New York: McGraw-Hill.

Cosmides, L., & Tooby, J. (1995). Beyond intuition and instinct blindness: Toward an evolutionarily rigorous cognitive science. In J. Mehler & S. Franck (Eds.), *Cognition on cognition* (pp.69-105). Amsterdam: Elsevier Science Publishers.

Dreier, O. (1999). Læring som ændring af personlig deltagelse i sociale kontekster. In K. Nielsen & S. Kvale (Eds.), *Mesterlære. Læring som social praksis* (pp.76-99). København: Hans Reitzels Forlag.

Ekman, P., & Friesen, W.V. (1971). Constants across culture in the face and emotion. *Journal of Personality and Social Psychology*, 17, 124-129.

Fischer, K., W., Ayoub, C., Singh, I., Noam, G., Maraganore, A., & Raya, P. (1997). Psychopathology as adaptive development along distinctive pathways. *Development and Psychopathology*, 9, 749-779.

Fog, J. (1985). Om den følsomme fornuft og den fornuftige følsomhed. *Psyke og Logos*, 6(1), 59-84.

Frith, U., & Happé, F. (1995). Autism: Beyond "Theory of mind". In J. Mehler & S. Franck (Eds.), *Cognition on cognition* (pp. 13-30). Amsterdam: Elsevier Science Publishers.

Gibson, J.J. (1986). *The ecological approach to visual perception*. London: Lawrence Erlbaum.

Harré, R. (1986) *The social construction of emotions*. Oxford: Blackwell.

Heard, D.H., & Barrett, M. (1982). Attachment and the family relationships of children with specific reading disability. In C. M. Parkes & J. Stevenson-

Hinde (Eds.), *The place of attachment in human behaviour* (pp. 151-167). London: Tavistock Publications.

Hundeide, K. (1985). The tacit background of children's judgments. In J.V. Wertsch (Ed.), *Culture, communication and cognition* (pp. 306-322). Cambridge: Cambridge University Press.

Hundeide, K. (1989). *Barns livsverden*. Oslo: J.W. Cappelens Forlag.

Johnson, M.H. (1997). *Developmental cognitive neuroscience*. Oxford: Blackwell.

Jordan, R. (1995). Teaching social skills without social understanding: The case of autism. In *Autisme '95* (pp. 2-26): Copenhagen: Ministry of Social Affairs.

Lave, J., & Wenger, E. (1991), *Situated learning – legitimate peripheral participation*. New York: Cambridge University Press.

Løvlie Schibbye, A-L. (2002). *En dialektisk relasjonsforståelse*. Oslo: Universitetsforlaget.

Macaulay, C. (2000). Transfer of learning. In V.E. Cree & C. Macaulay (Eds.), *Transfer of learning in professional and vocational education* (pp. 1-26). London: Routledge.

MacLean, P.D. (1985). Brain evolution relating to family, play, and the separation call. *Archives of General Psychiatry, 42*, 405-417.

Mammen, J. (1986). Erkendelse som objektrelation. *Psyke og Logos, 7*(1) 178-202.

McDermott, R.P. (1993). The acquisition of a child by a learning disability. In S. Chaklin & J. Lave (Eds.), *Understanding practice, perspectives on activity and context* (pp. 269-305). New York: Cambridge University Press.

McIntyre, R.B., Paulson, R.M., & Lord, C.G. (2003). Alleviating women's mathematics stereotype threat through salience of group achievements. *Journal of Experimental Social Psychology, 39*, 83-90.

Mead, G.H. (1934). *Mind, self and society*. Chicago: The University of Chicago Press.

Miller, G.A. (1956). The magical number seven, plus or minus two: Some limits on our capacity for processing information. *Psychological Review, 63*, 81-97.

Neisser, U. (1976). *Cognition and reality*. San Francisco: Freeman.

Niss, M., & Højgaard Jensen, T. (2002) *Kompetencer og matematiklæring*. Copenhagen: Ministry of Education.

Oatley, K., & Jenkins, J.M. (1996). *Understanding emotions*. Cambridge, MA.: Blackwell Publishers.

Olsen, B. (1999). Medlæring – et didaktisk perspektiv på uddannelsen af pædagoger. In S. Mossalski & P. Kirkegaard (Eds.), *Pædagogiske refleksioner* (pp. 207-228). Århus: Klim.

Reber, A.S. (1992). An evolutionary context for the cognitive unconscious. *Philosophical psychology, 5*(1), 33-51.

Rothbaum, F., Weisz, J.R., & Snyder, S.S. (1982). Changing the world and changing the self: A two-process model of perceived control. *Journal of Personality and Social Psychology, 42*(1), 5-37.

Schmader, T. (2002). Gender identification moderates stereotype threat effects on women's math performance. *Journal of Experimental Social Psychology, 38*, 194-201.

Smith, L. (1996). *Småbarnsalderens nevropsykologi*. Oslo: Universitetsforlaget.

Stern, D. (1995). *The motherhood constellation*. New York: BasicBooks.

Tanggaard Pedersen, L. (2004). *Læring og identitet i krydsfeltet mellem skole og praktik*. Unpublished doctoral dissertation. Aalborg: University of Aalborg.

Zajonc, R.B. (1980). Feeling and thinking. Preferences need no inferences. *American Psychologist, 35*(2), 151-175.